Millennium Redux

The Unstoppable Return of 2000s Trends

by

Aria Benson

Table of Contents

The 2000s Reawakened 1

Chapter 1: Echoes of a Millennium - The 2000s
Revival Phenomenon 4
    The Cultural Zeitgeist of the Early 21st Century 5
    Gen Z's Fascination with the 2000s 12

Chapter 2: Y2K Fashion on the Runway Again 15
    The Denim Revolution: Low Rise to Cargo Pants 16
    Accessorizing the 2000s: Layered Necklaces and Chunky Bracelets 19
    The Role of Social Media in Resurrecting 2000s Aesthetics 22

Chapter 3: The Beat Goes On - Music's Second Coming 26
    Pop Icons Revisited: Boy Bands and Pop Princesses 27
    The Mixtape Era: From CDs to Streaming Playlists 30
    Emo and Punk Rock: The Emotional Resonance with Gen Z 33

Chapter 4: Screen Time: TV and Movie Nostalgia 37
    The Sitcom Renaissance: From Friends to The Office 38
    Teen Dramas and Early Reality TV: A Cultural Study 41
    The Impact of Streaming Services on 2000s Revivals 44

Chapter 5: Gaming Reloaded - The 2000s Virtual Playground 48
    Console Wars: PlayStation 2 vs. Xbox 48
    The MMO Explosion: World of Warcraft and Beyond 52
    Mobile Games: The Evolution from Snake to Sophisticated Apps 55

Chapter 6: The Digital Revolution: Social Media's Origins 59

MySpace and the Rise of Personal Web Spaces 60

The Blogging Boom: LiveJournal and Blogger 63

Early YouTube: A Platform for Rising Stars 66

Chapter 7: Tech Trends Rebooted 70

Flip Phones to Smartphones: The Design Evolution 71

The MP3 Revolution: iPods and Portable Music 74

From AIM to Modern Messaging Apps: The Evolution of Online
Communication 77

Chapter 8: Beauty and Body Image in the 2000s................................. 81

Makeup and Hairstyles: Glitter and Straight Irons 82

The Fitness Craze: Celebrity Workout DVDs to Instagram Influencers............. 85

Addressing Body Image: Shifts Toward Inclusivity and Diversity 88

Chapter 9: The Rise, Fall, and Rise of 2000s Reality TV.................... 92

Survivor to The Simple Life: Reality as Entertainment 93

Competition Shows: Talent Uncovered 97

The Impact of Reality TV on Today's Social Media Culture 100

Chapter 10: 2000s Activism and Social Awareness: Then and Now 104

The Green Movement: Early Environmental Advocacy 105

Social Justice: From Awareness Campaigns to Hashtag Activism 108

The Influence of 2000s Activism on Modern Movements.....................112

Chapter 11: The Internet Culture: Memes, Virality, and Web
Communities... 116

The Birth of Memes: Impact on Communication 117

Viral Trends and Challenges: The Double-Edged Sword 120

Niche Communities and the Early Forums: Finding a Tribe Online 123

Chapter 12: The Future of the 2000s: What Comes Next? 127

Sustainability: Reinterpreting 2000s Trends with a Green Twist 128

The Cyclical Nature of Culture: Predicting the Next Big Revival.....................131

Gen Z and Millennials: Bridging the Past with the Future 134

Chapter 13: Millennium Redux - Embracing the Past,
Influencing the Future 138

Appendix A: Resources for 2000s Culture Enthusiasts 142
    Reading List 142
    Online Archives and Websites 143
    Social Media Accounts and Hashtags to Follow 143
    Reading List 144
    Online Archives and Websites 147
    Social Media Accounts and Hashtags to Follow 150

The 2000s Reawakened

The first decade of the new millennium, a vibrant era christened the 2000s, is experiencing a renaissance. A time once captured by the sound of dial-up internet and the glare of frosted lip gloss under club lights, it's making a bold, unabashed comeback. This revival, however, isn't merely a replication of the past; it's a reimagining for the future, melding nostalgic aesthetics with contemporary values.

The 2000s were a period of significant technological and cultural shifts. As we stood on the cusp of digital omnipresence, we also grappled with evolving fashion sensibilities, groundbreaking music genres, and the dawn of reality TV, not to mention the seismic shifts in global politics and social issues. It was a time of paradoxes—of both innocence and awareness, of looking forward while constantly being reminded of the past.

Today, as we delve into why the 2000s are being reawakened, it's essential to consider the context from which this resurgence springs. For millennials, the era evokes a tender nostalgia, a reminder of youth's simplicity and the excitement of a world growing increasingly connected. Meanwhile, Gen Z discovers these trends anew, interpreting them with modern twists that speak to current societal norms and values. Through this lens, the 2000s renaissance becomes a fascinating study of cultural recycling and adaptation.

This revival is not accident or coincidence; it's reflective of our longing for a time perceived as simpler, yet on the brink of technological revolution. The paradox lies in romanticizing an era that laid the groundwork for today's instant, digital world—while seeking refuge from that same world's relentlessness in nostalgia.

The fashion industry serves as a vivid illustration of this phenomenon, with Y2K styles like low-rise jeans and cargo pants strutting back onto runways and streets. These fashion statements are not mere repetitions but rather reinterpretations that echo the original spirit with a contemporary twist, addressing inclusivity and sustainability this time around.

Music from the 2000s, with its distinct blend of pop, alternative rock, and hip-hop, also finds new resonance today. Modern artists sample beats and themes from two decades ago, repackaging them for a generation that streams melodies on demand, demonstrating the timeless quality of the 2000s' sonic innovations.

Similarly, the realm of television and film has seen the return of iconic 2000s content, either rebooted for new audiences or celebrated in their original form on streaming platforms. This resurgence isn't just about reliving golden days but also about reevaluating and sometimes critically assessing the cultural narratives of the time.

The 2000s were also a pivotal era for gaming, marking the transition from niche hobby to mainstream entertainment. Today, the innovative spirit of 2000s gaming influences the design and storytelling of modern games, proving that the era's creative impulse continues to shape the future.

Perhaps nowhere is the 2000s' influence more evident than in the digital sphere, where social media and online communication began their ascent to ubiquity. The foundational platforms of the era laid the groundwork for today's digital networks, embedding elements of early internet culture in the DNA of current technologies.

When looking back at the 2000s' beauty trends—from glittery makeup to bold hair choices—it's clear that today's interpretations are more inclusive and diverse. This shift reflects a broader societal move towards embracing individuality and breaking down standards set by past decades.

Reality TV, a hallmark of 2000s television, has similarly evolved. Once a guilty pleasure, it's now a subject of academic study and critical discourse, acknowledging its impact on contemporary media landscapes and social norms.

The activism and social awareness seeded in the 2000s have blossomed into movements that leverage digital platforms to effect change, illustrating how the tools and attitudes of the era have empowered a new generation of advocates.

As memes and viral trends dominate our online spaces, it's worth recognizing the 2000s' role in shaping internet culture. The early forums and burgeoning web communities of the time paved the way for the expansive, interconnected digital ecosystem we navigate today.

Looking forward, the question isn't whether the 2000s will continue to influence us but how we will reinterpret its legacy through the prism of current and future challenges. In the cyclical nature of culture, the 2000s reawakened serve as a reminder that while time marches forward, the echoes of the past aren't merely echoes—they're conversations with the future.

Thus, as we embark on this journey through the reawakened 2000s, let's embrace the era's spirit with eyes wide open to the lessons it offers. It's a unique opportunity to blend nostalgia with innovation, to learn from the past as we pave the way for a new, exciting future.

Chapter 1:
Echoes of a Millennium -
The 2000s Revival Phenomenon

We've seen it unfold right before our eyes, a phenomenon that stretches across fashion runways, music playlists, and screen savers, echoing a bygone era with a modern twist. The 2000s revival has woven its way into the fabric of our current cultural landscape, rekindling a sense of nostalgia paired with a curious reinterpretation by those who first lived it and those who are encountering it anew. This chapter digs into the heart of why the early 21st century's peculiar mix of vibrant optimism and daunting complexity is resurfacing, compelling us to explore its undeniable influence on today's aesthetics and values. From the unmistakable sound of a modem connecting to the internet to the resurgence of cargo pants and flip phones, we're not just witnessing a cyclical return of trends; we're observing a nuanced revival that seeks to merge the unabashed boldness of the 2000s with today's evolving consciousness around identity, technology, and community. As we peel back the layers of this resurgence, we find that it's more than just an embrace of the past; it's a reimagining of the future through the lens of a time that felt both simpler and on the brink of technological revolution. Thus, this chapter sets the scene for a journey through the 2000s revival phenomenon, aiming to uncover not just the 'what' and the 'how,' but the 'why' behind this powerful cultural echo.

The Cultural Zeitgeist of the Early 21st Century

The early 2000s were not just a time of technological advancements and emerging digital frontiers but a period rich in cultural dynamism that echoed through the fashion, music, and lifestyle of a generation coming of age in a new millennium. Entrenched in the newfound freedom and possibilities that the internet promised, this era saw the culmination of 90s grunge evolving into a more polished yet daring aesthetic. The onset of reality TV reshaped traditional entertainment paradigms, encapsulating a society increasingly obsessed with celebrity culture and personal connectivity. Music, from pop to punk, became a vehicle for self-expression, with artists and fans alike exploring identity and societal issues through lyrics and community. Technology, on the cusp of the social media explosion, began altering the fabric of connection, setting the stage for a digital revolution that would influence everything from political movements to personal relationships. As we delve into the nuances of this period, it becomes clear that the early 2000s were not merely a preliminary chapter to the digital age but a foundational era that sculpted contemporary culture, inspiring a nostalgia that today's generations seek to recapture and reinterpret. With an eye towards understanding this pivotal time, we explore the myriad ways in which the 2000s continue to influence current trends, inviting a renaissance of ideas that resonate with both those who lived it and those discovering its legacy for the first time.

Fashion Fads and Flops In the whirlwind era of the 2000s, fashion trends were as unpredictable as they were bold. The turn of the millennium brought with it an explosion of styles that ranged from questionable choices to iconic looks that have cemented their place in the annals of fashion history. As we delve into the world of 2000s fashion, it's essential to remember that this decade was a time of experimentation, a period where fashion rules were broken, and personal expression was at its peak.

The 2000s saw the rise of what many might call fashion 'flops,' yet these very trends have made a surprising comeback in recent years. Take, for instance, the resurgence of low-rise jeans. Once a symbol of early 2000s pop culture, they were often criticized for being unflattering and uncomfortable. Today, however, they're being reimagined by designers and worn with a newfound confidence by a generation that's embracing body positivity and rejecting the notion that fashion should conform to a single body type.

Another notable trend was the abundance of accessories, with chunky, layered jewelry and belts that often served more aesthetic purposes than practical ones. While some might have viewed these as excessive at the time, they now represent a period of maximalist creativity that's influencing current accessory trends. This mix of nostalgia and innovation is leading to an exciting era of fashion that pays homage to the past while looking firmly toward the future.

The infamous 'flops' weren't just confined to clothing. The 2000s also introduced us to some bold beauty moves—from chunky highlights to frosted lip gloss—that were as daring as they were divisive. While they might have been met with skepticism, today's beauty standards are increasingly inclusive, allowing for more freedom to experiment and redefine what beauty means on an individual level.

One of the most polarizing pieces of the 2000s, however, had to be the trucker hat. A regular feature in the wardrobes of celebrities and teenagers alike, it epitomized the era's casual, laid-back approach to fashion. Its recent reappearance is a testament to the cyclical nature of fashion trends, proving that what goes out of style almost always comes back around.

The allure of early 2000s fashion lies not just in the clothing but in the attitude that accompanied it. It was a time of fearless self-expression, a moment when individuality was celebrated, and rules were made to be broken. This spirit resonates with today's generation, who are finding their voices and defining their identities in a world that's more connected than ever.

It's also worth noting the role of technology in propelling these trends back into the spotlight. Social media platforms have become digital archives of 2000s fashion, with influencers and fashion enthusiasts alike sharing their takes on these iconic looks. This accessibility has played a crucial role in the resurgence of trends that might otherwise have remained a distant memory.

The sustainability movement is bringing another dimension to the revival of 2000s fashion. Today's consumers are more conscious of the impact their clothing choices have on the environment. As a result, there's a growing interest in vintage and second-hand pieces from the 2000s, which are being repurposed and styled in innovative ways that reflect contemporary values.

In the realm of footwear, who could forget the platform flip flops and sneakers that defined a generation? Once considered a fashion faux pas, they're now embraced for their comfort and quirky appeal. This shift highlights a broader movement toward prioritizing comfort without compromising on style, aligning with the current emphasis on wellness and self-care.

The influence of 2000s pop culture on current fashion trends cannot be overstated. Iconic films, television shows, and music videos from the era serve as inspiration for designers and fashion enthusiasts, proving that the 2000s were more than just a decade of fashion mishaps; it was a rich cultural period that continues to influence the aesthetic choices of a new generation.

Moreover, the reimagining of 2000s fashion brings with it a sense of nostalgia that resonates deeply with Millennials. For many, these trends are not just clothing but memories of a simpler time, a connection to their youth. As such, the current revival is as much about recapturing the joy of those years as it is about the clothes themselves.

However, this resurgence is not merely a copy-paste of the past. Today's reinterpretations come with a twist, blending 2000s sensibilities with modern perspectives on inclusivity, sustainability, and technology. This hybrid approach is creating a fascinating dialogue between the past and the present, leading to innovative designs that respect their origins while pushing the boundaries of contemporary fashion.

The conversation around 2000s fashion - its fads and flops - is also a reflection of a broader societal shift. It's a manifestation of our desire to look back and learn from the past, to celebrate the journey that fashion has taken, and to acknowledge the strides we've made towards a more inclusive and conscious industry. As such, the revival of these trends is not just about aesthetics; it's a statement about the values and priorities of today's society.

As we continue to navigate the 21st century, the lessons learned from the 2000s fashion scene will undoubtedly play a crucial role in shaping the future of the industry. From embracing diversity to prioritizing sustainability, the impact of this era extends far beyond the clothes we wear. It's a reminder that fashion is not just about looking good; it's a powerful medium for expression, creativity, and change.

In conclusion, the 2000s fashion landscape was a testament to the creativity and diversity of the human spirit. As we revisit these trends, it's clear that what were once considered 'flops' have evolved into sources of inspiration, sparking a global conversation about identity, expression, and the future of fashion. In embracing the past, we unlock a wellspring of potential for innovation, proving that even the most maligned trends can find a second life in a new era.

Tech Evolution: From Dial-Up to Wi-Fi The journey from the screeching symphony of dial-up internet to the seamless connectivity of Wi-Fi encapsulates not just a technological leap but a cultural shift that redefined our social fabric. This transition was not merely about speed; it was about the transformation in how we interact, learn, and entertain ourselves. It's a narrative that's both nostalgic and instructive, offering a roadmap from our past innovations to future possibilities.

Reminiscing on the early days of dial-up internet evokes a sense of patience that seems almost alien in today's fast-paced digital world. The ritual of waiting for a connection, tied to a physical phone line, grounded our online adventures in the physical realm. This connection was not just slow by today's standards; it was a process, an event that required planning and patience. The anticipation built with each bleep and bloop until that triumphant moment of connection. It was a shared experience, a topic of conversation, and for many, their first taste of the digital frontier.

The limitations of dial-up were not just in speed but in accessibility. The internet was not always on; it was a resource that had to be shared and rationed, often leading to household negotiations and schedules. This scarcity of access made our online time precious, perhaps contributing to a more deliberate approach to internet use. Websites were simpler, less multimedia-rich, fostering a different kind of online creativity within those constraints.

As we transitioned to broadband and later Wi-Fi, the internet became a constant, pervasive presence. The shift to always-on connectivity represented a significant cultural shift. The internet was no longer a destination but a companion, a backdrop to our daily lives. This shift changed how we viewed and used the internet; it was no longer about going online but being online. The nature of online content exploded, with services like streaming video, online gaming, and social media becoming central to our digital lives.

Wi-Fi, in particular, untethered the internet from the confines of the home office or specific physical connections. It allowed the internet to permeate every corner of our homes and eventually, public spaces. This mobility transformed not just where we could access the internet but how we integrated it into our lives. It enabled new forms of digital nomadism, allowing people to work, learn, and play wherever they chose.

This evolution has had profound implications for social interactions. The advent of social media, powered by the ubiquity of Wi-Fi, has redefined our social landscapes. Relationships, communities, and identities are now maintained and expressed in digital spaces. This constant connectivity has blurred the lines between online and offline selves, creating complex digital identities that mirror and sometimes overshadow physical ones.

The democratization of internet access through Wi-Fi has been pivotal in educational and economic contexts. Information and opportunities that were once the preserve of a few are now accessible to many, leveling the playing field in unprecedented ways. This connectivity has ushered in an era of remote learning and work, dismantling traditional geographic and socio-economic barriers.

However, this transition has not been without challenges. The digital divide, the gap between those with effective access to digital and information technology and those without, has become more pronounced. As essential services and resources move online, those without reliable internet access find themselves at a disadvantage, highlighting the need for continued investment in digital infrastructure and literacy.

The environmental impact of our digital evolution is another area of concern. The energy demands of data centers, networks, and devices have grown exponentially, raising questions about sustainability and the environmental cost of our digital consumption. It prompts a critical examination of how we can balance the benefits of connectivity with its ecological footprint.

Looking ahead, the evolution from dial-up to Wi-Fi is a chapter in a larger narrative of digital transformation. The next frontier, from 5G to the Internet of Things (IoT), promises even greater connectivity and integration of digital technology into our physical world. As we stand on this threshold, reflecting on our journey helps us navigate the challenges and opportunities that lie ahead.

Understanding the evolution from dial-up to Wi-Fi also offers insights into the cyclical nature of technology and culture. Just as the 2000s saw a nostalgic revival of fashion and music from decades past, today's digital natives are rediscovering and reinterpreting the early internet's aesthetics and ethos. This resurgence of interest in the early digital era reflects a longing for a simpler online experience, perhaps less saturated with commercialism and more focused on genuine connection.

The journey from dial-up to Wi-Fi is a testament to human ingenuity and adaptability. It's a story of overcoming limitations and embracing possibilities, a narrative that resonates with anyone who has witnessed and navigated these changes. This evolution is a reminder that technology is not just about gadgets and speed; it's about the way we connect with each other and the world around us.

As we continue to navigate the digital age, the lessons from this transition from dial-up to Wi-Fi are clear. Embracing change, fostering inclusivity, and balancing innovation with sustainability are principles that will guide us as we forge new digital frontiers. It's a journey that's far from over, but one that offers endless possibilities for reimagining our digital futures.

In sum, the shift from dial-up to Wi-Fi is more than a technical upgrade; it's a cultural paradigm that has reshaped every aspect of our lives. The early internet's legacy, with its quirks and limitations, informs our understanding of digital connectivity and its impact on society. As we look to the future, we carry forward the spirit of innovation and community that has defined the digital age from its inception. It's a journey of transformation, one that continues to shape our world in profound and unpredictable ways.

Gen Z's Fascination with the 2000s

As we dive deeper into the heart of the 2000s revival, it becomes increasingly clear that Gen Z's obsession with this era is more than a fleeting trend. It's a complex amalgamation of nostalgia, curiosity, and a yearning for the simplicity that characterized the early days of the new millennium. This fascination is not just about reliving the past; it's about reimagining it for a new generation.

The 2000s were a time of rapid technological advances, from the emergence of social media to the dominance of MP3 players. For Gen Z, born on the cusp of this digital explosion, there's a natural intrigue around the devices and platforms that paved the way for their current digital playground.

Moreover, the era's fashion has seen a remarkable resurgence among this demographic. Low-rise jeans, cargo pants, and butterfly clips — once deemed outdated — are now celebrated for their bold defiance of today's minimalist trends. Gen Z has embraced these styles, not merely as vintage finds but as statements of individuality and self-expression.

Music from the 2000s, with its eclectic mix of pop, punk, and everything in between, holds a special place in the hearts of today's youth. The rise of streaming services has made it easier than ever for Gen Z to explore the discographies of artists who were once the staple of burned CDs and iPod Shuffles. This accessibility bridges the gap between generations, creating a shared musical landscape that transcends age.

The cultural output of the 2000s, from iconic TV shows to groundbreaking films, continues to influence Gen Z. Series like "Friends" and "The Office" experience renewed popularity as they find a home on streaming platforms, introducing a new audience to the humor, challenges, and aspirations of a decade gone by.

This generation's attraction to the 2000s extends beyond mere aesthetics or entertainment; it's also a reflection of their search for identity in an increasingly complex world. The early 2000s, while not without their challenges, are often viewed through rose-tinted glasses as a time of relative optimism and simplicity.

For Gen Z, the 2000s revival is also a form of escapism. Amidst the pressures of modern life, the early aughts represent a period of pre-social media innocence, where life's pace felt slower, and the world seemed smaller. This nostalgia is less about wanting to return to that time and more about capturing its essence in today's context.

However, it's crucial to recognize that this fascination goes beyond nostalgia. It's about making a statement in the present. By incorporating 2000s trends into their lives, Gen Z is challenging current norms and creating a hybrid culture that fuses the past with their vision for the future.

The environmental perspective also plays a significant role in this revival. Thrift shopping and upcycling, prominent among Gen Z, align with the sustainability ethos. Many see the adoption of 2000s fashion and tech as a form of eco-conscious consumption, breathing new life into items that would otherwise be forgotten.

On a deeper level, this resurgence is a form of cultural recycling, where old trends are reevaluated and repurposed to fit contemporary values. Gen Z's engagement with the 2000s highlights their ability to find harmony between nostalgia and progress, championing a future where the past serves as a foundation rather than a constraint.

Understanding this generation's fascination with the 2000s also offers insights into their collective psyche. It reveals a desire for connectivity in a digitally fragmented world. By embracing the culture, technology, and aesthetics of a bygone era, they're forging a communal identity that transcends the digital divide.

The 2000s revival, spearheaded by Gen Z, reflects a broader societal shift towards valuing authenticity, creativity, and sustainability. This movement is not merely about revisiting the past; it's about reshaping it to inspire a future where diversity of thought and expression is not just accepted but celebrated.

What's particularly interesting is how this nostalgia-driven trend influences the current market. Brands and industries are taking note, reintroducing products and concepts from the 2000s with a modern twist, thus blurring the lines between past and present.

This cyclical nature of culture, where trends come and go, underscores the dynamic relationship between generations and their cultural inheritances. In the case of Gen Z and the 2000s, it's a vivid illustration of how the old becomes new again, not just in style but in substance.

As we continue to explore the multifaceted dimensions of the 2000s revival, it's clear that this era holds a unique place in our collective memory. For Gen Z, it's not just a period to mimic or mythologize but a canvas on which they're actively painting their legacy. It's a testament to the enduring power of cultural nostalgia to not only connect us to our past but to also pave the way for innovation and inclusivity in the narratives we choose to celebrate.

Chapter 2:
Y2K Fashion on the Runway Again

In a dazzling turn of events that none of us saw coming, the Millennium has made its grand reentrance, taking the fashion world by storm in a way that's both nostalgic and refreshingly new. Y2K fashion isn't just making a comeback; it's being reinvented, repurposed, and reimagined by a generation that's both reliving their youth and discovering these trends for the first time. Designers have once again started mining the early 2000s for inspiration, sending models down the runway in outfits that scream Y2K—from metallic finishes and futuristic accessories to the revival of cargo pants and denim in forms that blur the lines between casual and couture. This resurgence isn't just a trip down memory lane; it's a statement. It speaks to the cyclical nature of fashion, yes, but also to a deeper desire among us to merge the aesthetic values of the past with the progressive ideals of the present. Through social media, this blend of old and new has found fertile ground, allowing people around the globe to engage with and reinterpret 2000s fashion in ways that resonate with contemporary values while still paying homage to the quintessential styles that defined a generation. This chapter delves deep into how and why Y2K fashion is dominating the runways again, exploring the cultural and social factors that have fueled its resurgence and examining how the current reinterpretation is more than just a fashion revival—it's a movement.

The Denim Revolution: Low Rise to Cargo Pants

The turn of the millennium wasn't just a shift in years; it signaled the dawn of a new era in fashion, spearheaded by the denim revolution. As we dive deeper into this exploration of Y2K fashion's resurgence, it's clear that the denim trends of the early 2000s have not just returned—they've evolved. From the controversial low-rise jeans to the utilitarian cargo pants, we're witnessing a revival that's as much about reclaiming the past as it is about setting new trends.

Low-rise jeans, once a staple of every pop star's wardrobe, epitomized the rebellious spirit of the early 2000s. They represented a shift towards a more relaxed, albeit provocative, aesthetic. Today, these jeans are making a comeback on the runway, but with a twist. They've been reimagined to fit a more inclusive range of body types, symbolizing not just a return to a bold fashion choice but a step forward in body positivity.

But the denim revolution doesn't stop at low-rise jeans. It extends to cargo pants, which have transcended their military origins to become a symbol of Y2K fashion's practicality and streetwear appeal. The cargo pants of today, seen on runways and streets alike, echo the past but are designed with modern fabrics and fits that appeal to contemporary tastes.

This renaissance of denim is more than a nostalgia trip; it's a conversation between generations. The millennials who first donned these trends are now viewing them through the lens of experience, while Gen Z is discovering them afresh, both drawn to the aesthetic appeal and the cultural significance behind each piece.

Incorporating denim into today's wardrobe isn't just about recreating looks from two decades ago. It's about remixing them, giving them new life and meaning. Designers are taking cues from the past but are conscious of the present's ethos, focusing on sustainability and ethical production. This reflects a broader shift towards a more thoughtful consumption of fashion, where the stories behind the clothes become as important as their looks.

The comeback of these denim trends is also a testament to the enduring appeal of comfort and functionality in fashion. Cargo pants, with their multiple pockets and relaxed fit, cater to the needs of today's on-the-go lifestyle, while the evolving design of low-rise jeans reflects an understanding of the diverse shapes and sizes of the human body.

What's particularly fascinating about the return of these trends is how social media has played a pivotal role. Platforms like Instagram and TikTok have become virtual runways, where users not only showcase their reinterpretations of Y2K denim but also engage in dialogues about fashion's impact on identity and society. This digital conversation is pushing the denim revolution into new territories, where individual expression and collective memory intersect.

The revival of Y2K fashion trends, particularly in denim, is not happening in a vacuum. It's part of a larger trend of 2000s aesthetics making a comeback, from pop culture references in music and TV to the resurgence of tech gadgets that defined the era. This interconnectedness of trends speaks to a collective yearning for a time that seemed simpler, yet it's also a recognition of the period's cultural significance.

Yet, as we embrace these trends, it's crucial to reflect on the lessons learned since they first emerged. The fashion industry's impact on the environment, the importance of inclusivity in design, and the ethics of production are all factors that today's consumers weigh more heavily. The denim revolution offers an opportunity to not only reimagine these iconic styles but to do so responsibly and thoughtfully.

Furthermore, the resurgence of cargo pants and low-rise jeans is redefining what it means to be fashionable. Once seen as relics of a bygone era, they're now symbols of a fashion-forward attitude that values both form and function. This shift is encouraging individuals to explore their personal style without being confined to the rigid standards of the past.

As we continue to navigate the evolving landscape of Y2K fashion, the denim revolution stands out as a vibrant example of how the past can inform the future. It's a blend of innovation and reflection, a dialogue between generations that's writing a new chapter in the history of fashion.

In the grand tapestry of fashion's evolution, the denim revolution of the early 2000s is a colorful thread woven with defiance, innovation, and a dash of nostalgia. Its resurgence on the runway and in everyday wear is not just a fleeting fad but a meaningful movement that encapsulates the spirit of an era while pushing towards a more inclusive and conscious future.

Indeed, the journey from low-rise jeans to cargo pants is more than a fashion statement. It's a reflection of our collective cultural journey, a testament to the power of clothing to capture the essence of an era, and a beacon for where we can go when we blend the best of the past with the hopes and values of the present. As we embrace the denim revolution once again, we're not just wearing clothes; we're wearing stories, memories, and the promise of a future where fashion is for everyone, regardless of their shape, size, or background.

In conclusion, the denim revolution of the 2000s and its resurgence today is a microcosm of the broader Y2K fashion revival. It encapsulates the essence of an era marked by bold choices and cultural shifts, serving as a bridge between the millennials who lived it and the Gen Z'ers who are reinterpreting it. In this denim story, we find a narrative of progress, a testament to the enduring power of fashion to inspire, challenge, and unite.

Accessorizing the 2000s: Layered Necklaces and Chunky Bracelets

The early 2000s were a time when fashion was not just about the clothes you wore but how you accessorized them. As we delve into the realm of Y2K fashion making a triumphant return to the runway, it's impossible not to spotlight two iconic trends that defined the era: layered necklaces and chunky bracelets. This resurgence isn't merely a replication of past trends; it's a reinterpretation that speaks volumes to a new generation eager to merge historical aesthetics with modern sensibilities.

Layered necklaces in the 2000s were often a mix of delicate chains, charms, and pendants that adorned the necks of trendsetters. They ranged from metallic finishes to colorful beads, each layer telling a story or showcasing a facet of the wearer's personality. Today, this trend echoes through the halls of fashion with a renewed vigor, tailored yet again to express individuality, but with a hint of nostalgia for an era admired by many.

Chunky bracelets, on the other hand, were the arm candy of choice for a generation looking to make bold statements. Be it wide cuff bracelets, stacks of bangles, or oversized beaded wristlets, these accessories were impossible to miss. In the current fashion landscape, these pieces have found new life, embodying the fearless spirit of the 2000s while embracing inclusivity and diversity in design and representation.

The allure of these accessories is not just in their aesthetic appeal but in their ability to elevate an outfit from mundane to extraordinary. They were, and are, tools of transformation, enabling wearers to curate their looks with precision and flair. The layered necklaces of today are more than just jewelry; they're a form of self-expression, a way for individuals to narrate their stories through the art of accessorizing.

Similarly, chunky bracelets have transcended their initial appeal to become symbols of strength and boldness. They're no longer just accessories; they're statements. In today's fashion scene, they reflect a growing desire for empowerment and a nod to the fearless fashionistas of the 2000s who wore their hearts on their sleeves... or rather, their wrists.

The process of accessorizing in the 2000s was also a testament to the era's experimental nature. Mixing metals, combining different jewelry styles, and layering pieces of varying lengths and sizes were practices that encouraged creativity and personal style. This experimental spirit is alive and well in today's fashion, championed by a generation that values authenticity and self-expression above all.

One can't discuss the resurgence of these trends without acknowledging the role of social media. Platforms like Instagram and TikTok have become modern-day runways, showcasing how layered necklaces and chunky bracelets are styled by trendsetters around the world. This global stage has not only breathed new life into these trends but has also facilitated a cross-cultural exchange of fashion ideas, further enriching the way we perceive and wear accessories.

The emotional resonance of 2000s accessories with today's audience is significant. For many, they evoke a sense of nostalgia, a longing for simpler times. For others, particularly those discovering these trends anew, they offer a fresh lens through which to explore and experiment with their style. This emotional dimension adds depth to the resurgence, making it more than just a revival; it's a celebration of an era that shaped a generation.

In the context of sustainability, the return of these accessories is also a boon. Many are turning to vintage and second-hand pieces, breathing new life into pre-loved necklaces and bracelets. This approach not only pays homage to the original era but also aligns with contemporary values of environmental consciousness and responsible consumption.

Furthermore, the resurgence of these trends is a reflection of the cyclical nature of fashion. It reinforces the idea that styles from the past can find relevance in the present, albeit with a modern twist. The 2000s accessorizing trends, with their emphasis on personalization and bold expression, are a perfect fit for a generation that values both individuality and inclusivity.

As these trends continue to evolve, they serve as a bridge between the past and the future. By embracing the layered necklaces and chunky bracelets of the 2000s, the fashion world is not just recapturing the essence of a bygone era but is also paving the way for new interpretations and innovations. It's a testament to the enduring influence of 2000s fashion and its capacity to inspire and resonate across generations.

The conversation around these accessories is also expanding to include discussions on craftsmanship, quality, and the stories behind the pieces. It's no longer just about the visual appeal but the values and narratives encapsulated in each piece, further enriching the trend's significance and impact.

In conclusion, the resurgence of layered necklaces and chunky bracelets is more than a fleeting fashion moment. It's a vibrant chapter in the ongoing story of 2000s fashion, reinterpreted by a generation that is keenly aware of its past yet eager to forge its own path forward. These accessories, with their rich history and contemporary appeal, symbolize a movement that celebrates creativity, diversity, and sustainability—a fitting tribute to the enduring legacy of Y2K fashion.

The return of 2000s accessorizing trends highlights a broader cultural phenomenon: a renaissance of nostalgia, reimagined for a new era. As fashion continues to evolve, the lessons from the past serve as stepping stones for future innovations. In embracing the layered necklaces and chunky bracelets of the 2000s, we're not just revisiting a trend; we're weaving a new narrative that bridges the gap between yesterday's charm and tomorrow's vision.

The Role of Social Media in Resurrecting 2000s Aesthetics

In the digital age, the resurgence of 2000s fashion is undeniably intertwined with the power of social media. Platforms such as Instagram, TikTok, and Pinterest have become pivotal in reintroducing the distinct aesthetics of the early millennium to a new generation. Through a blend of nostalgia, creative exploration, and digital connectivity, social media has transformed Y2K fashion from a mere memory into a dynamic and influential force on the runway once again.

At the heart of this revival is the visual-centric nature of social media. Instagram, with its emphasis on imagery, has allowed users to curate feeds that reflect their personal style, heavily inspired by iconic 2000s trends. Whether it's the resurgence of cargo pants, butterfly clips, or metallic eyeshadows, each post acts as a testament to the decade's enduring appeal. This visual storytelling extends to TikTok, where users not only showcase their attire but also create content that pays homage to the era's music videos and pop culture moments, further cementing the 2000s aesthetic in modern fashion.

Moreover, social media has democratized fashion, granting a platform to voices that were once sidelined. Diverse creators now lead the narrative, showcasing how 2000s trends can be adapted to fit a wide range of body types, ethnicities, and personal styles. This inclusivity is something that was often amiss in the original era, and it's inspiring to see it blossom as the aesthetics make their comeback. It emphasizes that while the trends may echo the past, their interpretation is firmly rooted in the values of today.

TikTok, in particular, has played a crucial role in this resurgence by facilitating a cross-generational dialogue. Gen Z creators, who may have been too young or not yet born to experience the decade first-hand, are often introduced to Y2K fashion by millennials who lived through it. This exchange fosters a unique blend of authenticity and reinterpretation, allowing the aesthetics to evolve while staying true to their roots. It's a beautiful example of how fashion cycles can bring people together, transcending age and time.

Pinterest serves as an ever-expanding digital mood board, where users pin their favorite 2000s looks, and draw inspiration for their wardrobe. The platform's algorithm cleverly suggests similar styles, creating an echo chamber of Y2K aesthetics. This not only aids in the discovery of new trends but also helps in tracking the evolution of 2000s fashion as it adapts to current tastes.

The role of influencers and celebrities cannot be overstated when discussing the resurgence of 2000s fashion on social media. High-profile figures with a penchant for nostalgic styles often spark significant interest in their followers. When a celebrity dons a vintage Juicy Couture tracksuit or accessorizes with a Von Dutch hat, it can quickly become a viral moment, leading to a resurgence of these iconic items. Their vast platforms offer visibility that can instantly reignite interest in trends that might otherwise have been forgotten.

Another facet of social media fueling the Y2K revival is the emphasis on sustainability. The 2000s were known for fast fashion, but today's fashion enthusiasts are keen on reducing waste. Thrifting and upcycling, popularized through social media platforms, echo the era's distinctive styles, proving that sustainability and nostalgia can coexist. This approach not only preserves the essence of 2000s fashion but also aligns with contemporary values regarding environmental responsibility.

User-generated content on social media also serves as a platform for experimentation, with individuals remixing 2000s trends with contemporary fashion to create hybrid styles. This blending of eras results in a fresh, innovative look that pays homage to the past while remaining ahead of its time. It's a testament to the era's adaptability and enduring influence on fashion.

The rapid spread of trends through social media hashtags has made 2000s aesthetics accessible to a global audience. Tags like #Y2KFashion or #2000sNostalgia aggregate content from around the world, showcasing the universal appeal of the era's style. This global conversation not only amplifies the trend but also incorporates diverse interpretations, enriching the Y2K revival with multiple cultural perspectives.

Finally, social media has become a powerful archival tool. Platforms are filled with collections of 2000s fashion editorials, runway shows, and celebrity outfits, acting as a digital museum of the era. This accessibility to the past provides an endless well of inspiration for those looking to recreate or draw from Y2K styles, ensuring the longevity of the trend.

In conclusion, the symbiotic relationship between social media and 2000s fashion has led to a dynamic resurgence of the era's aesthetics. This revival is not a mere replication but an evolution, shaped by contemporary values and technologies. As platforms evolve and new ones emerge, the influence of social media on fashion will undoubtedly continue to grow, breathing new life into the beloved trends of the past. The 2000s resurgence is a vibrant example of how fashion can bridge generations, cultures, and epochs—turning back the clock while marching boldly forward.

Through a mix of nostalgia, innovation, and community, social media has not just resurrected 2000s aesthetics; it has redefined them for a new era. The digital landscape has provided a fertile ground for exploration, allowing the past and present to converge in exciting, unexpected ways. As we continue to navigate the ever-changing world of fashion, the role of social media in shaping trends and connecting communities remains a powerful testament to its transformative impact. In embracing the past, we find clues to the future—a future that honors our collective histories while forging ahead into uncharted territories.

Therefore, as we deck ourselves in the relics of the early aughts, let us remember that fashion is not just about clothes—it's about expression, identity, and the endless cycle of rebirth. The 2000s revival serves as a vivid reminder of the enduring power of style to encapsulate eras, evoke memories, and inspire new generations. And in this digital age, we're all contributors to the ongoing story of fashion, weaving together threads of the past and present to create the tapestry of tomorrow.

Chapter 3:
The Beat Goes On - Music's Second Coming

The early 2000s were a defining era for music, marked by the emergence of genre-defining icons, groundbreaking albums, and the rise of digital music platforms. As we delve into "The Beat Goes On - Music's Second Coming," it's impossible not to feel a surge of nostalgia mixed with genuine excitement for how these tunes have found their way back to the forefront of our cultural consciousness. This resurgence isn't merely a replay of old hits but an intricate reweaving of the sonic fabric that defined a generation, now being embraced by a demographic that wasn't even born at the peak of its popularity. From the pop anthems that had us singing into our hairbrushes to the emo tracks that colored our teenage angst, the music of the 2000s never really left us; it just waited in the wings, ready for its second act. In this era of streaming, where discovery is as easy as the click of a button, these icons and anthems find new life, infusing the playlists of the modern listener with a sense of nostalgia and discovery. Whether it's the vinyl revival or the playlist curation on streaming giants, the essence of the 2000s is pulsating through our headphones and speakers, proving that the beat, indeed, goes on. This chapter not only explores the musical rebirth but also connects the dots between the timeless appeal of early 2000s music and its enduring impact on a generation that craves authentic connections in a digital age. As this music's second coming unfolds, it's clear that the magic of the 2000s is not just captured in the notes and rhythms but in the shared memories and emotions that these songs evoke, bridging the past and present in a melody that resonates across generations.

Pop Icons Revisited: Boy Bands and Pop Princesses

The early 2000s were a time of musical extravagance, an era where pop music's glossy finish met the burgeoning rise of digital media, creating icons that would define a generation. As we dive deep into our cultural nostalgia, it's impossible not to shine a light on the resurgence of the boy bands and pop princesses phenomenon. This was more than just catchy tunes; it was a global movement that now, in an age of digital streaming and social media dominance, millennials and Gen Z alike are rediscovering and redefining with a modern twist.

During their heyday, boy bands and pop princesses were more than just musicians; they were the epitome of pop culture. Groups like *NSYNC and the Backstreet Boys, along with solo acts like Britney Spears and Christina Aguilera, filled the airwaves and our hearts with their dance-worthy beats and heartfelt ballads. Their appeal wasn't just in their music but in their personas, meticulously crafted by the music industry, yet undeniably captivating. They were trendsetters in fashion, dialogues in teen magazines, and regular faces on MTV.

Fast forward to today, and the allure of these pop icons hasn't waned. Instead, it has evolved. With the power of social media, fans old and new have facilitated a renaissance, bringing back the soundtracks of the early 2000s with a fervor that matches, if not surpasses, the original craze. Platforms like TikTok, YouTube, and Spotify serve as the new MTV, allowing for a direct connection between artists and fans, fostering a community that transcends geographical boundaries.

What's fascinating about this revival is not just the nostalgia but how today's youth are interacting with it. Gen Z, many of whom were too young to experience the craze the first time around, are now among the most ardent supporters. For them, these artists and their music are not relics but rediscovered treasures, appreciated not just for their catchy melodies but for their place in cultural history.

The resurgence of vinyl and the explosion of playlist culture have also played significant roles in this phenomenon. Vinyl records, with their warm sound and tangible connection to the past, have become coveted items for collectors and new fans alike, further cementing the lasting impact of these pop icons. Meanwhile, curated playlists on streaming services allow fans to create their own mixtapes of sorts, blending old hits with new tunes, creating a personal soundtrack that spans decades.

This blend of old and new is perhaps most evident in the music itself. Modern pop artists openly draw inspiration from their early 2000s counterparts, incorporating elements of their sound, style, and even fashion into today's music scenes. This has led to an interesting fusion of genres, a blend of nostalgic sounds with contemporary themes that speak to a wide audience.

The influence extends beyond the music. Fashion trends spearheaded by these pop icons are returning, with Y2K fashion becoming a prominent trend among young people. The distinctive styles of low-rise jeans, bedazzled accessories, and bold prints are seen on runways and street corners, proving the lasting influence of these pop phenomena.

Moreover, the empowerment narrative that many pop princesses championed in their music resonates strongly today. Songs that were once dismissed as bubblegum pop are now heralded for their messages of independence and strength, reflecting a shift in societal values toward greater gender equality and self-expression.

The conversation about mental health, sparked by the very public struggles of some of these stars, has also taken a new dimension. Fans and critics alike are revisiting the past with a more empathetic lens, understanding the pressures faced by these young artists in the limelight and fostering a more supportive fan culture.

In the classroom and on social media, discussions about the cultural impact of these artists, and the era they dominated, are prevalent. Educators and influencers alike are dissecting the music, videos, and public personas of these pop icons, engaging in meaningful dialogues about celebrity, consumerism, and the evolution of pop music.

One cannot overlook the community aspect of this resurgence. Fan clubs and forums that were once the lifeline of fandom culture have found a new home in the digital space. Online communities thrive, sharing concert footage, rare recordings, and fan art, keeping the spirit of early 2000s pop alive and well.

This renaissance is not just about looking back; it's about moving forward with a sense of unity and appreciation for a time that, for many, was formative. It's a powerful reminder of music's ability to bridge the past and present, bringing together individuals of all ages to celebrate a shared love for an era that, though gone, is far from forgotten.

As we delve into this second coming of boy bands and pop princesses, it's important to recognize that this isn't merely a phase or a fleeting trend. It's a celebration of an era that shaped a generation, offering insights into how cultural phenomena can evolve and endure. In embracing the past, we pave the way for a future where the beat, indeed, goes on.

The enduring appeal of these early 2000s icons speaks volumes about the cyclical nature of pop culture. As trends ebb and flow, the foundational elements of what captivates us remain constant: relatable lyrics, infectious beats, and charismatic personalities. In reexamining the pop icons of the early 2000s, we don't just reminisce; we rediscover the essence of what makes pop music truly timeless.

In the end, the resurgence of boy bands and pop princesses is more than a testament to their lasting impact on music and culture. It's a beacon for future generations, illustrating the power of nostalgia, the importance of community, and the unifying force of music. As the beat goes on, we remain eager participants in this ongoing dialogue between the past and the present, forever shaped by the icons who soundtracked our lives.

The Mixtape Era: From CDs to Streaming Playlists

In the vibrant tapestry of 2000s music culture, mixtapes held a special place in the hearts of those who lived through it. This wasn't just about music; it was about the personal touch, the craftsmanship of curating a playlist that could define a moment, a relationship, or an era. The transition from physical CDs to streaming playlists marks not only a technological evolution but a shift in how we interact with and relate to music.

At the heart of the mixtape era was the CD, a tangible object that could be held, gifted, and treasured. Crafting a mix CD was a labor of love, from choosing the right songs to arranging them in an order that told a story or set a mood. The act of giving a mix CD was personal, often a gesture of friendship or budding romance. The recipient would insert the mix into their CD player, and the carefully selected tracks would fill their space, each song carrying the curator's intentions and emotions.

However, as the digital age dawned, music began to shed its physical form. With the rise of MP3 players and later smartphones, music became more about accessibility and less about the artifact. This transition laid the groundwork for streaming services, which would eventually transform mixtapes from a physical collection of tracks into digital playlists.

The essence of the mixtape survived this technological overhaul, emerging in the form of streaming playlists. Platforms like Spotify and Apple Music became the new canvas for musical curation, allowing users to craft playlists with the same intent and personality as the mix CDs of the past. The creation became easier, yes, but the underlying purpose remained: to convey a message through music.

Streaming playlists also democratized music curation. No longer were people limited by their own CD collections or the need for physical materials. Anyone with an internet connection could now create and share a playlist, reaching audiences far beyond their immediate social circle. This access has led to a renaissance in music sharing, where playlists are crafted for every occasion, mood, and moment.

Yet, with this ease of access came a sense of impermanence. The digital nature of modern playlists, while convenient, lacks the tactile feel of handling a CD. The excitement of writing down the tracklist by hand, of decorating the CD cover, has been replaced by a few clicks and taps on a screen. The gesture remains heartfelt, but the physical connection to the music has faded.

Moreover, the art of discovery has changed. In the era of mix CDs, finding a new song or artist often came through friends or painstaking searches through music stores. Now, algorithms and automated "Recommended for You" playlists attempt to predict our tastes, altering the serendipity of stumbling upon an unknown band or track.

Despite these changes, the mixtape's essence persists in the digital age. Playlists have become a common language, a way to communicate feelings, share experiences, and connect with others. They're used in much the same way mixtapes were, as gifts, as stories, as memories. The method of delivery has evolved, but the heart of the mixtape era beats on.

What's fascinating is how this transition from CDs to streaming has impacted music itself. Artists and producers now consider how songs will fit into playlists, possibly affecting everything from track length to genre blending. The mixtape mentality has infused the very creation of music, emphasizing tracks that can stand alone or be part of a larger, curated experience.

Additionally, the rise of streaming playlists has led to new forms of social interaction. Sharing a playlist online can connect people across the globe, forging communities around specific genres, moods, or even activities. This global exchange of music has made the world both larger and more intimate, expanding our musical horizons while reminding us of the universal language of melody and rhythm.

However, the nostalgia for mix CDs and their tangible connection continues to inspire a resurgence of physical media in music. Vinyl records have made a significant comeback, and even cassettes have seen a renaissance among collectors and enthusiasts. This longing for the physical suggests that while the format may change, the desire to connect through music, to own something that holds our personal history, remains strong.

As we move forward, the mixtape era's legacy is one of creativity, connection, and personal expression through music. It taught a generation the value of curating soundtracks for our lives and the power of music to capture the essence of our most profound experiences and emotions. The medium has changed, but the mixtape's spirit continues to inspire and influence how we share the songs that resonate with us the most.

Ultimately, the transition from CDs to streaming playlists is more than just a shift in technology; it's a chapter in the ongoing story of how we relate to music. It's a testament to music's enduring power to bring us together, to express what words alone cannot, and to soundtrack the moments that define us.

In embracing the streaming age while honoring the mixtape era's roots, we're weaving a rich tapestry of musical tradition that spans generations. We're not just listening to music; we're participating in a cultural exchange that encompasses the past, present, and future. The beat goes on, and in every playlist we craft, the mixtape's soul lives on, adapting to new forms but always retaining its essence of personal touch and emotional connection.

As we continue to navigate the digital landscape, let's not forget the mixtape era's lessons: that music is a means of connection, a vessel for our stories, and a bridge between hearts. In every playlist we create and share, we're keeping the spirit of the mixtape alive, celebrating the joy of discovery and the timeless art of curation. The mixtape era, from CDs to streaming playlists, reminds us that regardless of the format, music will always be a reflection of our shared humanity.

Emo and Punk Rock: The Emotional Resonance with Gen Z

As we delve deeper into the sonic resurgence of the 2000s, it becomes increasingly evident that the revival isn't just about the melodies or the rhythms; it's about the raw, unfiltered emotion embedded in the music of that era. Emo and punk rock, in particular, are experiencing a monumental comeback, reaching out and gripping the hearts of Generation Z with a fervor comparable to that of their millennial predecessors. This affinity between Gen Z and the emotionally charged aspects of these genres offers a profound insight into the collective psyche of today's youth.

Emo music, with its introspective lyrics and confessional style, carved out a significant niche in the early 2000s. Bands like My

Chemical Romance, Fall Out Boy, and Panic! At The Disco provided a soundtrack to the angst and existential turmoil of a generation. These bands, with their poetic dissections of personal and emotional conflicts, became more than just artists; they were the voice for those who felt misunderstood, sidelined, or simply overwhelmed by the rigors of teenage life.

On the other side of the spectrum, punk rock, with its roots in rebellion and societal critique, continued to evolve from its 1970s origins into the 2000s, echoing a disdain for the status quo and championing the cause of individuality. Bands like Green Day and Blink-182 addressed themes of disillusionment, suburban angst, and the yearning for escape, themes that resonated deeply with their listeners.

Fast forward to today, and it's clear why these genres are resonating with Gen Z. In an age marked by rapid technological change, political instability, and a pandemic that has fundamentally altered the fabric of daily life, the themes of emotional turmoil, existential angst, and societal critique are more relevant than ever. The resurgence of emo and punk rock is not merely a nostalgic trip down memory lane; it's a reaffirmation of their enduring relevance.

Gen Z's embrace of these genres is facilitated, in part, by social media and streaming platforms. Unlike the millennials, who had to rely on mix CDs or downloads to discover new music, today's youth have the world's discography at their fingertips. Platforms like Spotify and YouTube offer personalized recommendations, allowing users to explore deep cuts and new iterations of their favorite 2000s genres. TikTok, in particular, has played a pivotal role in this revival, with users creating and sharing content that pairs emo and punk rock tracks with contemporary cultural commentary, fashion, and humor.

The visual aesthetic of emo and punk rock, characterized by distinctive fashion choices such as skinny jeans, band tees, studded belts, and an overall embrace of the "alternative," has also seen a revival. This re-emergence demonstrates the cyclical nature of fashion trends and how they often go hand-in-hand with musical movements. For many Gen Z'ers, adopting this style is a form of self-expression and an ode to a bygone era they wish they'd experienced firsthand.

Moreover, the themes of mental health awareness and emotional vulnerability, hallmarks of the emo genre, align closely with Gen Z's values. This generation is marked by its willingness to open up about mental health struggles and its advocacy for emotional transparency. The emo revival, therefore, is not just about the music; it's about the message and its relevance in today's socio-cultural landscape.

Importantly, today's artists are not just replicating the sound of the early 2000s; they are redefining it. Bands and musicians influenced by the original waves of emo and punk are infusing the genres with contemporary sensibilities, addressing modern-day themes such as social justice, identity, and the experience of growing up in the digital age. The result is a rich, evolved sound that pays homage to its roots while charting new territory.

This revival also speaks to the power of music as a cultural bridge. In rediscovering the anthems of their older siblings or even their parents, Gen Z finds common ground with the generations that preceded them. Conversations about emo and punk rock bands become a point of connection, a shared language in a world often divided by generational misunderstandings.

As emo and punk rock continue to resonate with Gen Z, it's clear that the appeal of these genres goes beyond mere nostalgia. It's about a continuous search for identity, a quest for meaning, and a need for community. The music of the 2000s provided a haven for those grappling with the complexities of life, and today, it serves a similar purpose for a new generation.

The emotional resonance of emo and punk rock with Gen Z is a testament to the timeless nature of music. It's a reminder that, regardless of the era, music has the power to validate our feelings, challenge the status quo, and bring us together. As we look to the future, the enduring legacy of these genres will undoubtedly continue to evolve, inspire, and comfort listeners, old and new.

In the grand tapestry of music history, the return of emo and punk rock is more than a trend; it's a movement. It's a resurgence of heartfelt expression, a revival of passionate dissent, and, most importantly, a beacon of hope for those searching for their place in the world. The beat indeed goes on, with each chord and chorus echoing the universal quest for understanding, acceptance, and connection.

As we continue to witness the second coming of music's most emotionally charged genres, let us remember the power of a song to heal, to unite, and to inspire. Emo and punk rock have found a new home with Gen Z, and in this rediscovery, a generation finds its voice, its battle cry, and its anthem for navigating the complexities of the modern world.

The story of emo and punk rock's resurgence is far from over. As these genres evolve and adapt, they promise to remain a vital part of the cultural conversation, offering solace, solidarity, and strength to those who listen. In this symphony of the past and the present, we find a hopeful note for the future, a reminder that in times of turmoil, music remains our most resilient and unifying force.

Chapter 4:
Screen Time: TV and Movie Nostalgia

In this journey through the 2000s, "Screen Time: TV and Movie Nostalgia" stands out as not just a chapter but as a portal into the moments that shaped a generation's expectations of entertainment, love, friendship, and the complexity of life's dramas. As we dive into the world of sitcoms that redefined laughter, friendship, and workplace dynamics, it's evident how series like 'Friends' and 'The Office' have not just entertained but provided a blueprint for relationships that resonate across generations. The surge of teen dramas and early reality TV challenged norms, shaped aspirations, and provided a gritty mirror to the complexity of adolescence, all the while being consumed on boxy TVs and later, glossy flat screens. Now, with the advent of streaming services, these cultural icons have been resurrected, allowing a new generation to debate on 'Ross and Rachel' or marvel at the ingenuity of 'Punk'd'. This digital renaissance not only brings nostalgia to those who lived it but also invites Gen Z into a dialog with the past, weaving their contemporary perspective into the fabric of 2000s TV and movie lore. As we look at the screen through the lens of today, we're reminded that these shows and films were more than just entertainment; they were the backdrop of our lives, teaching, amusing, and inspiring us in ways that are being rediscovered and reimagined today. In reflecting on this era's unique blend of humor, drama, and reality, we understand why its revival is not just about looking back, but about carrying forward the essence of a time that continues to shape our contemporary culture and societal values.

The Sitcom Renaissance: From Friends to The Office

As we delve into the heart of TV and movie nostalgia, a very special chapter must be dedicated to the era's sitcom renaissance, spanning iconic shows like *Friends* to *The Office*. This period encapsulates a transformation in American television, molding the comedic landscape for years to come. These shows didn't just entertain; they became cultural touchstones, shaping our perceptions of friendship, love, and office dynamics, all while wrapping the lessons in humor and heart.

Friends, debuting in the mid-'90s and running until the mid-2000s, tapped into the essence of young adulthood, navigating life's ups and downs together. It wasn't just about the laughs; it was about seeing ourselves in each of the characters, their struggles and triumphs imitating our own. The wit, charm, and delightful chemistry amongst the cast carved a template for sitcom success.

Transitioning from Central Perk to Scranton, Pennsylvania, *The Office* introduced us to a mockumentary style that brought viewers closer to the Dunder Mifflin crew than ever thought possible. Beyond its groundbreaking format, it was the show's understated commentary on the mundanities of office life and its eccentric yet endearing characters that captured audiences' hearts. Michael Scott's misguided but well-intentioned leadership, Jim and Pam's slow-burning romance, Dwight's unparalleled idiosyncrasies—all of these elements worked in concert to make *The Office* a beacon of 2000s TV.

The success of these shows can't be discussed without acknowledging their departure from traditional sitcom frameworks. Single-camera setups, lack of live audience laughter in *The Office*, and a focus on character development over canned punchlines symbolized a shift in storytelling techniques. This evolution resonated with viewers seeking authenticity and depth in their comedic consumption.

Moreover, the cultural impact of these sitcoms extends beyond their original run. The proliferation of streaming services has granted these shows a second life, introducing them to new generations. *Friends* and *The Office* routinely top the charts as the most-watched shows on platforms like Netflix, proving their timeless appeal. This resurgence is a testament to their relatability, humor, and warmth that continue to enchant audiences worldwide.

The thematic richness of both series provides fodder for endless discussions — from the evolution of workplace culture reflected in *The Office* to the changing dynamics of relationships and family seen in *Friends*. These discussions are not just nostalgic revisits but also critical examinations of how far we have come and where society stands today in comparison to the turn of the millennium.

An essential component of these shows' legacies is how they've influenced modern sitcoms. The DNA of *Friends* and *The Office* can be seen in numerous shows that followed, from the ensemble camaraderie of *Parks and Recreation* to the life-and-love explorations in *How I Met Your Mother*. Current series borrow from their playbook, blending humor with human emotion and everyday relatability, capturing the essence of what made their predecessors so captivating.

The question of why these shows from the 2000s continue to resonate deeply with both Millennials and Gen Z can be partly answered through the lens of escapism and the search for genuine connections. In an era where digital interactions often replace face-to-face connections, *Friends* and *The Office* offer a return to a seemingly simpler time. They present a world where personal interactions drive the narrative, reminding us of the value of human connection.

Furthermore, the humor and situations in these shows, while sometimes veering into the absurd, are grounded in universal truths about life's unpredictability and the importance of finding joy amid chaos. This blend of escapism, reflection, and genuine human connection provides a comforting balm that continually attracts viewers.

The global fan communities that have sprung up around *Friends* and *The Office* further amplify their cultural significance. From online forums to social media accounts dedicated to quoting every line, these communities keep the spirit of the shows alive. They serve not only as a bastion for fans to share their favorite moments but also as a space for new viewers to discover the magic that made these sitcoms so beloved in the first place.

It's also worth noting the role of nostalgia in the enduring appeal of these shows. For many, rewatching episodes is akin to revisiting old friends, a comforting and familiar experience that evokes fond memories of the past. This emotional resonance, combined with the timeless quality of the storytelling, ensures that these shows remain relevant and loved.

Looking ahead, the legacy of *Friends* and *The Office* in television history is secure. They've set high bars for character development, comedic timing, and cultural impact, offering blueprints on how to touch the hearts and tickle the funny bones of audiences worldwide. As we continue to see revivals and reboots in the entertainment industry, the question isn't whether these shows will remain relevant— they've already proven they will. Instead, we should ask how future generations will reinterpret these classics for the modern era, keeping the essence alive while adapting to new cultural landscapes.

Ultimately, the sitcom renaissance of the 2000s, spearheaded by shows like *Friends* and *The Office*, represents more than just a peak in comedic television. It symbolizes the power of storytelling to connect, comfort, and inspire across generations. As we move forward, embracing new trends and technologies, let's not forget the lessons these shows taught us about laughter, love, and the beauty of human connection.

In examining the threads that weave through our cultural fabric, it's clear that the impact of these sitcoms extends beyond mere entertainment. They challenge us to reflect on our lives, relationships, and societal norms. Their enduring popularity underscores a universal truth: amid changing times, the quest for connection, understanding, and a good laugh remains constant. So, as we celebrate the sitcom renaissance of the 2000s, let's carry its spirit forward, allowing it to illuminate our paths as we navigate the complexities of the modern world.

Teen Dramas and Early Reality TV: A Cultural Study

At the turn of the millennium, television was in the throes of a significant transformation. Teen dramas and early reality TV shows were not just filling up the programming slots; they were creating a new lexicon of pop culture phenomena. This era set the stage for narratives and archetypes that would define a generation's social and cultural attitudes.

Teen dramas of the early 2000s, such as "Dawson's Creek," "The O.C.," and "Gilmore Girls," crafted a landscape filled with idyllic small towns and picturesque high schools, where every teenager seemed embroiled in a Shakespearean level of personal conflict. These shows, with their complex characters and equally complex relationships, served as a mirror to the angst, aspirations, and the tumultuous journey of coming of age. Through their narratives, they tapped into the universal themes of love, friendship, and the quest for identity, engaging their audience in a deep, sometimes cathartic dialogue.

Meanwhile, early reality TV was rewriting the rules of engagement for viewers. Shows like "Survivor," "Big Brother," and "The Real

World" introduced audiences to a form of entertainment that was unscripted, unpredictable, and utterly raw. These programs not only challenged perceptions of what television content could be but also how viewers saw themselves and others. The allure of watching real people navigate extraordinary situations or the mundanity of daily life in a fishbowl environment was irresistible.

The juxtaposition of teen dramas with their crafted narratives against the ostensibly 'unfiltered' reality shows presented a diverse tapestry of storytelling. These genres, in their unique ways, offered viewers an escape while also holding up a mirror to their realities, desires, and fears.

These shows became the backdrop against which a generation formulated its understanding of relationships, morality, and personal identity. Teen dramas, with their elaborate story arcs, taught lessons in resilience, the importance of connections, and the pain of loss. Reality TV, on the other hand, offered a reflection on social dynamics, the allure of fame, and the concept of 'reality' in entertainment.

The influence of these shows extends beyond their airtime into the fabric of online culture. Forums and fan sites allowed viewers to dissect episodes, share theories, and forge communities. This collective engagement marked the beginning of fandom culture as we know it today, setting the stage for how current generations engage with content on digital platforms.

Moreover, the portrayal of technology, fashion, and music in these shows captured the zeitgeist of the era, creating a nostalgic lens through which we view the early 2000s. The omnipresence of flip phones, the evolution of indie rock, and the trends that swept through the corridors of fictional high schools reflected and influenced real-life trends.

The enduring appeal of 2000s teen dramas and reality TV can be attributed to their exploration of timeless themes through a contemporary lens. As new generations discover these shows, they find resonance in the universal experiences of adolescence and the human condition, despite the changing societal context.

The recent resurgence in popularity of these genres, fuelled by streaming platforms and social media, is testament to their lasting impact. Millennials revisiting the shows of their youth and Gen Z discovering them anew are not just indulging in nostalgia but are engaging in a dialogue with the past to understand their present.

This intergenerational exchange underscores the cyclical nature of culture. As 2000s aesthetics and sensibilities are reinterpreted by a new generation, they are imbued with contemporary values, creating a dynamic fusion of the past and present.

The legacy of 2000s teen dramas and reality TV is thus not merely in their entertainment value but in their role as cultural artifacts that continue to shape societal narratives. They serve as a window into the complexities of human emotion and social interaction, exploring themes that are as relevant today as they were two decades ago.

It's clear that the cultural study of teen dramas and early reality TV offers rich insights into the social fabric of the early 21st century. By examining these shows, we not only reminisce about a bygone era but also understand more deeply the cultural threads that connect us across generations.

In conclusion, the significance of teen dramas and early reality TV in shaping our collective consciousness cannot be understated. They stand as pillars of pop culture history, offering endless material for analysis and reflection. As we look to the future, we carry with us the lessons, aesthetics, and narratives of the past, ready to be reexamined and reborn for a new generation eager to make their mark.

So, as we navigate the burgeoning waves of 2000s revival, let us remember the role these shows have played in our cultural landscape. They remind us that, even as the world changes, the stories we tell and consume continue to shape who we are, inspire us, and connect us in ways we're only beginning to understand.

The Impact of Streaming Services on 2000s Revivals

In the digital age, where the line between the past and the present blurs, streaming services have emerged as time machines capable of catapulting us back to the 2000s. This chapter delves into how platforms like Netflix, Hulu, and Amazon Prime have been instrumental in the resurgence of 2000s TV shows and movies, thus playing a significant role in the ongoing cultural renaissance of the era.

The convenience of streaming services has transformed the viewing experience, making it easier than ever to access content from any period. This accessibility has allowed newer generations to discover titles from the 2000s, which, in turn, has sparked interest in the fashion, slang, and lifestyle of the era. For millennials, it's a walk down memory lane, reigniting the nostalgia for their youth. For Gen Z, it's an exploration of the cultural artifacts that shaped the societal norms they live by today.

Shows like "Friends," "The Office," and "Gilmore Girls" have enjoyed a second life on streaming platforms, introducing them to viewers who were too young to appreciate them during their original runs. These revivals aren't just about reliving the glory days; they reflect a deeper desire to connect with simpler times. The pre-social media era, depicted in these shows, offers a compelling contrast to today's always-connected, digital-first lifestyle, making them surprisingly relevant.

Streaming services have not only made it easier to revisit beloved 2000s content but have also paved the way for reboots and sequels. Series like "Gilmore Girls: A Year in the Life" and "Fuller House" were directly influenced by the popularity of their originals on streaming platforms, showcasing the demand for new content that retains the charm and appeal of its predecessors.

Moreover, the impact of these services extends beyond just TV shows. Movies like "Mean Girls" and "The Princess Diaries" have found a new audience, further fueling the 2000s revival. This resurgence has influenced fashion trends, language, and even attitudes, as younger viewers adopt elements from these early 2000s classics into their own lives.

Streaming platforms have also played a crucial role in the music industry's nostalgia wave, with soundtracks from 2000s movies and series making their way onto modern playlists. These platforms provide a space for the era's iconic music videos and concert footage, connecting fans old and new with the sounds of the decade.

The revival of 2000s content has sparked conversations about the era's cultural significance and its influence on today's society. Through panels, podcasts, and social media discussions, fans and critics alike delve into the themes, styles, and societal norms reflected in these shows and movies, unpacking their relevance and lessons for contemporary audiences.

However, this revival also prompts a critical examination of the 2000s through a modern lens. Streaming services offer an opportunity to address and discuss issues related to gender, race, and sexuality that were often glossed over at the time. This has led to a more nuanced appreciation of these works, recognizing their flaws while celebrating their contributions to pop culture.

The economics of streaming services has influenced the television and movie production landscape, encouraging creators to develop content that resonates with both nostalgia-seekers and new audiences. This has led to a blending of genres, styles, and themes from the 2000s with contemporary storytelling techniques, creating a unique fusion that appeals to a broad viewer base.

This resurgence is not just a fleeting trend but a testament to the lasting impact of the 2000s on modern culture. Streaming services have facilitated a bridge between generations, allowing them to share experiences, discuss differences, and find common ground in the stories that define a decade.

As streaming platforms continue to dominate the entertainment industry, their role in shaping cultural trends and revivals is undeniable. They have become curators of history, offering a gateway to the past while paving the way for future innovations in storytelling and media consumption.

The 2000s revival, powered by streaming services, reflects a broader movement towards embracing nostalgia as a source of comfort, inspiration, and connection. It's a reminder that the past can offer valuable insights into the future, encouraging us to look back with fondness as we move forward.

For those fascinated by the cultural and technological nostalgia of the 2000s, this era's revival is more than just a trip down memory lane; it's an opportunity to understand how yesterday's trends are being reinterpreted by a new generation. Through streaming services, we're not only reliving the 2000s but reimagining them for a future that merges past aesthetics with contemporary values.

In conclusion, the impact of streaming services on 2000s revivals is a multifaceted phenomenon that has redefined how we engage with past, present, and future media. It's a testament to the power of nostalgia, the evolution of technology, and the ever-changing landscape of pop culture. As we continue to explore the depths of the 2000s, streaming services will undoubtedly remain at the forefront of this cultural journey, reminding us that some things are indeed timeless.

Chapter 5:
Gaming Reloaded - The 2000s Virtual Playground

As the dawn of the 21st century broke, the gaming world found itself at the cusp of a digital renaissance, a period that would forever alter the landscape of interactive entertainment. In the heart of this transformation was the emergence of console wars, with PlayStation 2 and Xbox vying for domination, their rivalry igniting a fervor amongst gamers that was both unprecedented and exhilarating. This era wasn't just about hardware, though; it witnessed the MMO explosion, led by behemoths like World of Warcraft, which crafted virtual realms that transcended the games themselves, becoming cultural phenomena that offered both escape and identity. Meanwhile, on the mobile front, the progression from the simplicity of Snake to the sophistication of apps demonstrated not just technological advancement but a change in the very way we conceived of gaming's place in our daily lives. These weren't merely games; they were gateways to vast, unexplored digital playgrounds, offering endless possibilities that beckoned the imagination to wander, compete, and connect. The 2000s didn't just redefine gaming; they redefined our connection to the digital world, reminding us that within the circuitry and code lay the potential for adventure, creativity, and camaraderie.

Console Wars: PlayStation 2 vs. Xbox

The early 2000s marked a pivotal moment in the gaming industry, a period that could only be described as the golden age of console gaming. At the heart of this era were two giants vying for dominance: Sony's PlayStation 2 (PS2) and Microsoft's Xbox. This battle not only shaped the future of gaming but also left an indelible mark on the cultural landscape of the 2000s.

Released in 2000, the PS2 quickly became a household name, boasting an impressive lineup of games and backward compatibility with its predecessor, the PlayStation. Its early entry into the market gave it a significant head start, capturing the hearts of gamers worldwide. The PS2 wasn't just a gaming console; it was a multimedia hub that played DVDs, which at the time were a burgeoning format, adding a layer of attractiveness for the non-gaming demographic.

In contrast, Microsoft's Xbox, which launched in 2001, brought something new to the table: a built-in hard drive. This innovation was a game-changer, allowing for downloadable content, a feature that's now standard in the industry. The Xbox also boasted superior graphics capabilities compared to the PS2, along with the introduction of Xbox Live, laying the groundwork for online multiplayer gaming that has since become a staple.

The rivalry between these two consoles was more than just a competition of hardware. It was a battle of exclusives, a war waged through iconic titles that would define a generation. Sony had juggernauts like "Grand Theft Auto: San Andreas," "Final Fantasy X," and "Shadow of the Colossus," while Microsoft countered with "Halo: Combat Evolved," "Fable," and "Forza Motorsport." These games were not just entertainment; they were cultural phenomena, pushing the boundaries of what video games could be and inspiring a generation of gamers.

Yet, this console war was about more than the games or the technology. It was a reflection of the changing landscape of entertainment, where video games began to rival movies and music as a dominant form of pop culture. The early 2000s saw video games transition from niche hobby to mainstream, with the PS2 and Xbox playing crucial roles in this shift.

The impact of this console war extends beyond nostalgia. It set the stage for the future of gaming, laying the foundations for online play, digital distribution, and the integration of multimedia capabilities into gaming consoles. The battles between the PS2 and Xbox were not just about the here and now; they were about shaping what gaming would become.

Moreover, the rivalry fostered a sense of community among gamers. Forums and early social media were ablaze with debates over which console was superior. Friendships were formed over shared loyalties, and the competition drove innovation, pushing each company to continually improve and innovate.

In the end, the PS2 emerged as the best-selling console of its generation, securing its place in the annals of gaming history. However, the Xbox carved out its niche, building a foundation upon which Microsoft would continue to grow its gaming division, setting the stage for its future endeavors in the industry.

Looking back, it's clear that the console wars of the early 2000s played a pivotal role in the evolution of video gaming. They were about more than just two companies fighting for market share; they were about defining what video gaming could be and expanding its role in popular culture. The innovations and ideas born from this rivalry continue to influence the industry today.

The PlayStation 2 vs. Xbox rivalry is a fascinating chapter in the story of video gaming, one that highlights the power of competition to drive innovation and change. It's a narrative that's not just about technology but about the people who embraced these consoles, the communities that formed around them, and the lasting impact they've had on entertainment and culture.

As we look to the future, the legacy of the PS2 and Xbox rivalry teaches us an important lesson: that in the world of technology, competition spurs growth, creativity, and progress. The battles of yesterday lay the groundwork for the innovations of tomorrow, reminding us that in the quest for advancement, there are no true losers, only the relentless march forward.

For those of us who lived through this era, the console wars of the early 2000s hold a special place in our hearts. They represent a time of simplicity and discovery, a period when the potential of video gaming seemed boundless. We look back not just with nostalgia but with gratitude, for it was during these years that many of us discovered our passion for gaming.

To the new generation of gamers, the tales of the PS2 vs. Xbox might seem like ancient history. Yet, they offer invaluable lessons about where gaming has come from and where it's headed. As we stand on the brink of new technological frontiers, we carry forward the spirit of innovation, competition, and community that defined the console wars of the early 2000s. The battleground may have shifted, but the game goes on, fuelled by the same passion and enthusiasm that gave rise to the golden age of console gaming.

In sum, the PlayStation 2 vs. Xbox saga is a testament to the transformative power of video games. It reminds us that at the intersection of technology, culture, and community lie endless possibilities. As we forge ahead into new realms of virtual reality, cloud gaming, and beyond, we do so standing on the shoulders of giants, informed by the lessons of the past and inspired by the promise of the future.

The MMO Explosion: World of Warcraft and Beyond

The dawn of the 21st century brought with it not just technological advancements but a revolution in the way we engage with digital realms. In the heart of this digital renaissance was the Massive Multiplayer Online (MMO) game genre, with World of Warcraft (WoW) blazing trails and setting benchmarks. When WoW was released in 2004, it wasn't just a game; it became a phenomenon that transcended gaming culture, seeping into the fabric of mainstream media and conversations.

Imagine, if you will, a world where tens of millions of players from around the globe come together in a singular, expansive universe. This wasn't just about logging in to slay dragons or complete quests – it was about forging relationships, building communities, and in many cases, finding a place where one felt they belonged. WoW offered an escape but also a parallel reality where achievement, camaraderie, and the thrill of exploration were as tangible as in the 'real' world.

The explosion of MMOs in the 2000s wasn't just a testament to advancing internet capabilities or graphical prowess; it was a sign of the times. People were yearning for connections, for experiences that broke the mold of traditional gaming. WoW and its contemporaries paved the way for a virtual playground where imagination and interaction were limitless.

But the impact of WoW didn't plateau with its own success. It set off a chain reaction, inspiring a plethora of MMOs and even influencing other game genres. From Guild Wars to Final Fantasy XIV, developers took the blueprint that WoW laid out and ran with it, each creating vast worlds with their own unique lore, gameplay mechanics, and communities.

It's imperative to understand the cultural significance of this period. MMOs became a shared cultural touchstone for millions. They were discussed in schools, depicted in movies, and even used as platforms for social experiments. WoW and games like it were no longer just games; they were digital countries, with their own economies, politics, and social norms.

The 2000s also saw the rise of "gold farming" and the real-money trade of in-game assets, which highlighted the economic impact of MMOs. These practices, although controversial, demonstrated how virtual worlds were beginning to mirror our own, with economies that were just as complex and driven by supply and demand.

Then, there was the social aspect. MMOs created opportunities for people to connect in ways that were previously unimaginable. They brought together individuals from diverse backgrounds, facilitating friendships and even relationships that crossed geographical boundaries. The stereotype of gamers being isolated was challenged by the communal experiences offered by MMOs.

Education and research found a place in MMOs too. Educators explored virtual worlds as platforms for teaching and learning, while psychologists studied MMOs to understand more about human behavior, addiction, and the social dynamics of virtual communities.

As technology evolved, so did MMOs. They became more accessible, with some transitioning to free-to-play models, broadening their player base. This accessibility further embedded MMOs into the cultural lexicon, ensuring that they weren't just a fleeting trend but a staple of digital entertainment.

While WoW might have been the catalyst, the MMO genre's growth contributed significantly to the evolution of online gaming. It showcased the potential of the internet as a medium for immersive, interactive experiences and carved a path that future technologies, like virtual reality, would eventually tread upon.

However, the landscape wasn't devoid of challenges. As the novelty wore off, some MMOs struggled to retain players. The genre had to evolve, incorporating new elements like mobile gaming compatibility and integrating social media to maintain relevance in an ever-changing digital environment.

Today, as we look back on the MMO explosion of the 2000s, it's clear that its impact goes beyond entertainment. It fostered a generation that values connectivity, collaboration, and community. These values are now more pertinent than ever as we navigate an increasingly digital world, seeking meaningful interactions in virtual spaces.

World of Warcraft, and the MMO genre it helped define, acted as pioneers in the digital frontier. They showed us the power of virtual worlds to unite, entertain, and sometimes even educate. As we move forward, the legacy of the MMO explosion of the 2000s continues to influence not just gaming, but how we perceive and interact within digital spaces. It was a testament to human creativity and the desire for connection, proving that in a world of infinite possibilities, the need to come together, share experiences, and create stories is universal.

In a way, the MMO explosion encapsulated the essence of the 2000s digital playground. It was a time of exploration, of breaking down barriers, and most importantly, of building bridges. As we continue to advance technologically, the principles of community and shared experience that MMOs championed remain as vital as ever. They remind us that at the heart of every technological leap, the human element – the desire to connect, to escape, to play – underpins it all.

The echoes of the MMO explosion are still felt today as new generations discover these virtual worlds. The torch has been passed, but the flame of community, exploration, and adventure still burns brightly, illuminating the path for the future of gaming and beyond.

Mobile Games: The Evolution from Snake to Sophisticated Apps

Turning the pages back to the dawn of mobile gaming, we find ourselves in an era dominated by the iconic game Snake, which became a standard on Nokia phones. This pixelated adventure, where a line mimicking a snake eats dots to grow longer, didn't just capture our attention; it sparked a revolution. Its simplicity and addictiveness were a harbinger of the mobile gaming potential, setting the stage for the sophisticated apps we know today.

As we progressed into the 2000s, technological advancements were rapidly transforming the mobile gaming landscape. Phones evolved from mere communication tools to portable entertainment devices. Java games, though simplistic by modern standards, were a significant leap forward, offering a variety of genres from puzzles to strategy. This versatility showed us that mobile phones could provide diverse gaming experiences, laying the groundwork for future innovations.

The introduction of color screens and better graphics capabilities marked another milestone. Games began to boast improved visuals, which enriched the gaming experience. Titles like 'Bounce' and 'Space Impact' demonstrated that mobile games could have compelling aesthetics and gameplay, further solidifying their place in our daily lives.

However, it was the launch of the Apple App Store in 2008 that truly revolutionized mobile gaming. For the first time, developers had a unified platform to distribute their games, reaching an unprecedented audience. This democratization of game development opened the floodgates to a deluge of creativity and innovation.

Games like 'Angry Birds' and 'Fruit Ninja' became household names, synonymous with mobile gaming success. Their simple, touch-based controls and addictive gameplay made them instant classics, showcasing the potential for viral success in the mobile gaming market.

But beyond their entertainment value, these games represented a new era where mobile games became part of the mainstream gaming conversation.

As smartphones became more powerful, so did the games they could support. We began to see titles with graphics and complexity that rivaled those on consoles and PCs. Games like 'Infinity Blade' and 'Asphalt' series proved that mobile platforms could offer deep, visually stunning experiences, blurring the lines between mobile and traditional gaming.

The incorporation of online multiplayer and social features further evolved mobile gaming. Titles like 'Clash of Clans' and 'Words With Friends' created communities and competitive arenas, mirroring the social dynamics of console and PC gaming. This connectivity not only enhanced the gaming experience but also fostered a sense of community among players.

Free-to-play models and microtransactions, while controversial, were another turning point. They made games accessible to a broader audience, changing how developers monetized their creations. This model has its critics, but it's undeniably shaped the mobile gaming industry, influencing even the strategies of console and PC games.

The rise of augmented reality (AR) games like 'Pokémon GO' marked yet another transformation, merging the virtual and real worlds in ways previously unimaginable. This game, in particular, showed that mobile games could create mass social phenomena, bringing people together from all walks of life in shared digital and physical spaces.

Looking ahead, the future of mobile gaming is bound to be even more immersive with technologies like virtual reality (VR) and further advancements in AR. We're standing on the brink of experiencing games that could fully immerse us in alternate realities, accessible from the devices nestled in our pockets.

The evolution from Snake to today's sophisticated mobile apps encapsulates a journey of innovation and expansion that mirrors broader technological and societal shifts. It's a testament to how far we've come, from relishing in the simplicity of guiding a pixelated line across a screen to exploring complex virtual worlds with friends from around the globe.

Mobile gaming's trajectory reflects a democratization of gaming, making it accessible to everyone with a smartphone. This inclusivity has expanded the gaming community, welcoming players who might not have access to consoles or PCs. It's indicative of a broader trend towards technological empowerment, creating opportunities for play, creativity, and connection.

This journey also underscores the potential for future innovations to transform our daily lives. Just as mobile games evolved from simple diversions into complex experiences that can educate, connect, and inspire, so too can other technologies reshape our world in ways we're just beginning to imagine.

As we reflect on the evolution of mobile gaming, it's clear that its story is far from over. With each technological leap, developers will craft new worlds for us to explore, stories for us to inhabit, and challenges for us to overcome. The games of the future will continue to stretch the boundaries of what's possible, inviting us to play, learn, and grow in ways we can scarcely conceive of today.

In celebrating the transformation from Snake to sophisticated apps, we're not just reminiscing about the games themselves but also honoring the creativity, innovation, and spirit of play that drive us forward. As we look to the future, let's carry forward the lessons and joys from two decades of mobile gaming, eager to see where this journey takes us next.

Chapter 6:
The Digital Revolution: Social Media's Origins

In the early 2000s, a significant shift happened that forever changed how we connect, share, and view the world around us. This era heralded the dawn of the digital revolution, a period marked by the creation and explosive growth of social media platforms. Born out of a desire for connection in an increasingly digital world, platforms like MySpace allowed users to craft personal web spaces where they could express themselves in ways previously unimaginable. Meanwhile, blogging platforms such as LiveJournal and Blogger offered a diary-like outlet for sharing thoughts and adventures, creating the foundation for the influencers and content creators we know today. Then came early YouTube, a platform that revolutionized how we consume video content, turning ordinary people into rising stars overnight. These nascent stages of social media were not just technological innovations; they were the harbingers of a cultural shift. They democratized content creation, gave rise to new forms of celebrity, and reshaped our social interactions. As we revisit the 2000s, it's clear that understanding social media's origins isn't just about nostalgia; it's about grasping how these beginnings have influenced a generation to reinterpret and mold the digital world according to contemporary values. This chapter dives deep into the roots of the digital revolution, exploring how the early platforms set the stage for a world where everyone can be both creator and consumer, a legacy that continues to define the digital landscape today.

MySpace and the Rise of Personal Web Spaces

In the early 2000s, the internet landscape was dramatically transformed with the emergence of personal web spaces, with MySpace leading the charge. This platform wasn't just a website; it was a canvas for the digital self, where users could express their personalities, interests, and relationships in a multitude of colorful ways. The rise of MySpace marked a pivotal moment in the digital revolution, shaping the way people interacted online and laying the foundation for the social media era that would follow.

MySpace's introduction in 2003 was timely, coinciding with an era where internet connectivity began moving from luxury to necessity. It provided a platform that was uniquely positioned to tap into the cultural zeitgeist, combining music, social networking, and personal expression into one seamless experience. This trifecta appealed to a broad audience, from teenagers seeking to carve out their digital identity to artists and musicians looking to promote their work to a wider audience.

The personalization features of MySpace were revolutionary. Users could modify their profile's look with custom backgrounds, choose songs to play when visiting their page, and curate a top friends list. These features weren't just about showcasing one's digital presence; they were about establishing a personal brand in the nascent days of online social networking. This level of customization was unprecedented and became a hallmark of the MySpace experience, influencing many social media platforms that followed.

MySpace also played a critical role in democratizing content creation and distribution, particularly in the music industry. Unsigned bands and independent musicians used the platform to upload their music, connect with fans, and even get discovered by record labels. This broke down traditional barriers to entry in the music industry, allowing talent to be recognized based on popularity with the MySpace community rather than the whims of record executives. This democratization of music discovery paved the way for numerous success stories and shifted how the music industry searched for and promoted new talent.

At its peak, MySpace was a cultural phenomenon, embodying the ethos of the early 2000s digital culture. It was a place where friendships were formed, trends were set, and the seeds of today's influencer culture were sown. MySpace photos, with their distinct aesthetic and often peculiar angles, became iconic, capturing the essence of a generation coming of age online.

However, the digital landscape is ever-evolving, and the reign of MySpace wouldn't last indefinitely. The rise of Facebook, with its cleaner interface and focus on real-life connections, posed a significant challenge. As users migrated, MySpace struggled to retain its relevance and user base. This shift underscored the volatile nature of internet fame and the importance of innovation in maintaining market dominance.

Despite its decline, the legacy of MySpace in shaping social media cannot be understated. It introduced concepts such as the "friend request," which have become staples of digital interaction. It also showcased the power of community-driven content, laying the groundwork for the user-generated content models of platforms like YouTube, Instagram, and TikTok.

For many, MySpace was more than just an online platform; it was a critical part of their adolescent and early adult years. It offered a space for experimentation with identity, interests, and social circles in a way that had not been possible before. The nostalgia for MySpace is not just about the platform itself but what it represented—an era of internet innocence and exploration, before social media was woven into the fabric of everyday life.

The lessons learned from the rise and fall of MySpace are invaluable. They highlight the importance of adaptability, user focus, and innovation in the tech industry. MySpace taught us that even the most popular platforms could quickly become obsolete if they fail to evolve with their users' needs and expectations.

Today's social media giants owe a great deal to MySpace. It served as a proving ground for many features that are now taken for granted in social media design and functionality. The emphasis on user profiles, networking, and multimedia content has influenced the development of the platforms that dominate the digital space today.

As we look back on the influence of MySpace and the era of personal web spaces, it's clear that this period was just the beginning of a social media revolution that would transform communication, culture, and commerce. The principles of community, personal expression, and connectivity that MySpace championed continue to be at the heart of digital interaction.

In reflecting on MySpace's impact, it becomes evident that the platform was a key player in the digital revolution. It contributed significantly to the development of online culture and social networking, shaping the way individuals and communities interact online. The story of MySpace is a testament to the transformative power of technology and the internet, reminding us of the rapid pace of change and the constant evolution of digital spaces.

MySpace's history is a poignant reminder of the internet's fleeting nature. Yet, it also celebrates the spirit of innovation and the endless possibilities that arise when people connect online. As we continue to navigate the ever-changing landscape of social media, the lessons from MySpace and the era of personal web spaces offer enduring insights into the dynamics of digital culture and the human desire for connection and expression.

In conclusion, the rise of MySpace and personal web spaces marked a foundational chapter in the history of social media. It captured the imagination of a generation, set new trends in digital interaction, and paved the way for the future of online connection. As we move forward, the legacy of MySpace serves as a reminder of the power of innovation and the importance of embracing change, inspiring us to reimagine the possibilities of the digital age.

The Blogging Boom: LiveJournal and Blogger

In the constellation of the digital revolution that reshaped the early 2000s, two stars shone brightly, igniting the blogging boom that laid the groundwork for today's social media landscape. LiveJournal and Blogger emerged as pivotal platforms, offering users unprecedented ways to share their thoughts, experiences, and creativity with a global audience. This section delves into how these platforms catalyzed a cultural shift towards online expression and community building, influencing a generation and beyond.

LiveJournal, launched in 1999, was more than just a blogging platform; it was a social network ahead of its time, fostering a sense of connection and community among its users. The platform introduced features such as friends lists, allowing users to follow each other's journals and create a personalized feed of content. This aspect of social connectivity revolutionized the way people interacted online, moving beyond mere personal websites to a more interconnected web of stories and experiences.

Blogger, on the other hand, initiated by Pyra Labs in 1999 and later acquired by Google in 2003, democratized content creation like never before. It offered a user-friendly interface that made publishing on the web accessible to everyone, not just to those with technical know-how. Blogger empowered individuals to share their insights, hobbies, and personal narratives with a broader audience, paving the way for the influencers and content creators we see today.

One of the most transformative aspects of LiveJournal and Blogger was how they embraced the personal voice. Blogs became digital diaries, platforms for self-expression where writers could share their inner worlds—thoughts, feelings, and reflections—with authenticity and immediacy. This personal touch resonated with readers, who found solace, inspiration, and camaraderie in the words of strangers.

The rise of these blogging platforms coincided with significant global events, such as the turn of the millennium, the aftermath of 9/11, and the early stages of globalization. Writers used LiveJournal and Blogger to document their lives against this backdrop, offering personal perspectives on world events, contributing to a more nuanced and diverse media landscape.

Moreover, these platforms were instrumental in the early development of niche communities. Whether through shared interests in pop culture, fashion, technology, or social issues, bloggers found and cultivated their tribes. These communities offered support, validation, and a sense of belonging to many, especially to those who felt marginalized or misunderstood in their offline lives.

The blogging boom also heralded the age of citizen journalism, with bloggers often reporting on stories overlooked by mainstream media. From the front lines of protests to the personal impact of global crises, blogs became a source of alternative news and perspectives. This participatory media landscape prompted a more democratized form of information dissemination and consumption.

As we reflect on LiveJournal and Blogger's legacies, it's evident that they were more than just platforms; they were catalysts for a cultural movement towards openness, authenticity, and digital community building. They laid the foundation for the social media ecosystems we inhabit today, predating the likes of Facebook, Twitter, and Instagram.

It's also essential to recognize the challenges these platforms faced, including issues of privacy, online harassment, and the monetization of content. These issues, still relevant today, highlight the complexities of online life and the ongoing need for platforms that prioritize user safety and experience.

The evolution from blogging to today's social media is marked by changes in technology, user behavior, and cultural values. However, the essence of what made LiveJournal and Blogger revolutionary— giving a voice to the voiceless, fostering community, and democratizing content creation—remains at the heart of social media.

Looking to the future, the legacy of these pioneering platforms offers valuable lessons for the next generation of digital spaces. As we navigate the complexities of the online world, the principles of community, authenticity, and inclusivity that defined the blogging boom will continue to guide the evolution of social media.

For those of us who remember the early days of blogging, the nostalgia is not just for the platforms themselves but for the spirit of innovation and connection they embodied. As we witness the resurgence of 2000s trends across fashion, music, and technology, the blogging boom stands out as a testament to the enduring impact of early digital culture.

In the tapestry of the digital revolution, LiveJournal and Blogger hold a special place, reminding us of the power of sharing our stories with the world. As we move forward, their legacy inspires us to imagine new possibilities for creativity, community, and connection in the digital age.

As we continue to explore the origins and evolution of social media in this chapter, let us remember the role of LiveJournal and Blogger not just as platforms but as pioneers that paved the way for the dynamic and diverse digital landscape we enjoy today. Their story is a crucial chapter in understanding how we came to live, share, and connect online.

In conclusion, the blogging boom of the early 2000s, led by LiveJournal and Blogger, was a pivotal moment in the digital revolution. It shaped the way we think about online identity, community, and storytelling. As we look back, we're reminded of the power of individual voices coming together to create a global tapestry of shared experiences—a legacy that continues to influence the digital world.

Early YouTube: A Platform for Rising Stars

At the heart of the digital revolution that characterized the 2000s, there existed a platform that was about to redefine fame, creativity, and how stories were told. This platform was YouTube. Founded in 2005, YouTube began as a simple video-sharing website but quickly evolved into a stage for aspiring artists, comedians, and creators of all kinds. Its influence on culture and media cannot be overstated, as it offered an unprecedented opportunity for visibility and connection.

Unlike traditional media, YouTube's model was democratized; it didn't require one to have connections in the industry or an expensive portfolio to be seen. Instead, it asked for authenticity and creativity. This openness led to the birth of a new era of celebrities - "YouTubers." They were individuals who could command audiences that numbered in the millions, purely on the strength of their content.

One of the most compelling aspects of early YouTube was its capacity to serve as a platform for undiscovered talent. Musicians, in particular, found a home on YouTube, using it as a means to share cover songs, original compositions, and music videos. Artists like

Justin Bieber and Shawn Mendes are prime examples of how YouTube could catapult unknown musicians into the global spotlight nearly overnight.

But it wasn't just musicians who found fame through YouTube. Comedians, filmmakers, and educators also harnessed the platform to experiment with content and reach audiences far beyond their immediate geography. This gave rise to a new form of entertainment, one that was raw, unfiltered, and deeply personal. Creators weren't just faces on a screen; they were real people sharing real stories, which resonated with viewers on a personal level.

Among the sea of content, vloggers emerged as some of YouTube's biggest stars. They documented their daily lives, shared their thoughts on various topics, and invited viewers into their personal worlds. This genre of content wasn't polished or scripted, which was precisely its appeal. It was authentic and relatable, forging a genuine connection between creators and viewers.

The platform's global reach also meant that creators weren't limited by their geographic location. A YouTuber in Canada could become a sensation in Japan, while a British makeup artist could inspire viewers in Brazil. This global community fostered a sense of belonging and understanding among people from disparate backgrounds, making the world feel a bit smaller and more connected.

YouTube's influence extended beyond individual success stories. It changed how entertainment was consumed and created. Suddenly, anyone with a camera and an internet connection could contribute to the cultural zeitgeist, challenging traditional narratives and offering a diversity of perspectives and stories that were previously missing from mainstream media.

Moreover, the early days of YouTube played a crucial role in shaping internet culture. Memes, viral videos, and catchphrases born on the platform would go on to become part of the global lexicon, further illustrating YouTube's impact on popular culture.

As the platform grew, so did its features, with YouTube introducing monetization opportunities through ad revenue, sponsorships, and fan funding. This financial aspect allowed creators to turn their passion projects into careers, further professionalizing the space and attracting even more talent to the platform.

Education and learning found a unique home on YouTube as well. From DIY tutorials to lectures on quantum physics, the platform made knowledge accessible in a way that was both engaging and entertaining. It democratized learning, removing barriers to education and information.

Yet, with growth came challenges. Issues of copyright, content moderation, and creator burnout began to surface, signaling the complexities of managing a platform with such vast influence and reach. Despite these hurdles, YouTube's foundational years laid the groundwork for what it would become—a vital part of the digital landscape.

Today, as we look back, it's clear that early YouTube was more than just a collection of videos. It was a cultural movement that encapsulated the spirit of the 2000s—a time of exploration, innovation, and the breaking down of traditional barriers in media and entertainment. It was a testament to the power of digital technology to elevate everyday individuals into stardom, connect communities across the globe, and reshape the entertainment industry.

In reflecting on YouTube's legacy, it's evident that its early years were instrumental in defining the digital age. It enabled a generation of creators to express themselves, impact the world, and, in many ways, anticipate the future of content creation.

The rise of early YouTube serves as a reminder of the potential for technology to foster creativity, transform lives, and influence global culture. As we move forward, the lessons learned from YouTube's ascendancy continue to inspire new platforms and creators to innovate and dream big, pushing the boundaries of what's possible in the digital era.

In embracing the nostalgia of the 2000s, it's crucial to recognize platforms like YouTube, which not only shaped the decade but also set the stage for the future of entertainment and communication. Its legacy as a platform for rising stars endures, reminding us of a time when the world felt at our fingertips, ready to be explored and shared in just a click.

Chapter 7:
Tech Trends Rebooted

In the whirlwind evolution of technology, the new millennium's onset was marked by distinctive gadgets and digital phenomena that defined an era. "Tech Trends Rebooted" delves into the nostalgic embrace and ingenious reinvention of these iconic technologies by a generation equally enthralled by the charm of the past and the promise of the future. The journey from flip phones, which once symbolized the pinnacle of compact design and personal tech, to smartphones exemplifies how aesthetic and functionality are melded in modern devices, incorporating sleek designs with expansive capabilities that were unimaginable in the early 2000s. Meanwhile, the MP3 revolution, heralded by devices like the iPod, redefined music consumption, a concept further evolved today as streaming services offer the world's music at our fingertips. Perhaps most intriguing is the trajectory of online communication. From the simple text-based interfaces of AIM, we've transitioned to multifaceted messaging apps that not only allow instant communication across the globe but also support multimedia sharing, video calls, and even digital payments. Through a careful examination of these transitions, this chapter illuminates how present-day innovators draw from the past, not for mere replication but to craft technologies that resonate with modern values while evoking a sense of nostalgia. This exploration not only fosters an appreciation for the tech marvels of the 2000s but also inspires us to envision a future where innovation continues to pay homage to its roots.

Flip Phones to Smartphones: The Design Evolution

The transformation from flip phones to smartphones is arguably one of the most significant tech trends of the late 20th and early 21st centuries. It wasn't just about hardware or software—it was about reshaping how humanity communicates, works, and plays. Every aspect of our digital lives has been touched by this shift, making it a cornerstone of the modern technological landscape.

Flip phones, with their satisfying snap closure, compact design, and relatively simple interfaces, symbolized the height of mobile tech sophistication in the early 2000s. They were more than just devices; they were fashion statements, accessories that complemented one's personal style and signaled one's tech savvy. However, as revolutionary as they were, flip phones had limitations that would soon become apparent with the advent of their successors.

The introduction of smartphones marked a paradigm shift. The move from physical buttons to touchscreens was not just a change in input methods; it was a reimagining of human-device interaction. Smartphones melted away the boundaries between different forms of media, integrating phone calls, messaging, internet browsing, gaming, and photography into a single, sleek device that fit in the palm of your hand.

Consider the design evolution: early smartphones, while more versatile, were often bulkier and less intuitively designed than their flip phone predecessors. Yet, they offered possibilities that flip phones simply couldn't. Apps opened up a new world for developers and users alike, allowing for an unprecedented level of customization and functionality. This was a device that could learn and adapt to the user, rather than the user having to adapt to the device.

As smartphones evolved, they became thinner, faster, and more powerful. Their screens grew larger and clearer, with displays that made browsing the web and watching videos a pleasure rather than a strain. The design became more refined, with manufacturers painstakingly considering every curve, material, and feature.

This design evolution was driven by a push towards a more connected and seamless world. Smartphones broke down the barriers between online and offline, making digital a natural extension of our physical world. They've enabled new forms of social interaction, transforming not just how we communicate but who we can communicate with. The global village is now more than a metaphor; it's a reality, largely thanks to smartphones.

One can't overlook the impact of the app economy, which exploded in tandem with smartphone adoption. It's a realm that encouraged innovation and disruption, offering a platform for creators to reach a global audience with nothing but a great idea and some coding knowledge. This democratization of development has led to breakthroughs in everything from gaming to health care, finance to education.

However, the journey from flip phones to smartphones has not been without its concerns. Issues such as digital privacy, screen addiction, and the environmental impact of rapidly obsolete devices are more pressing than ever. These challenges remind us that innovation must be balanced with responsibility—a theme that resonates with the broader 2000s revival.

Nostalgia for flip phones, often seen through the lens of simplicity and disconnection, has spurred a minor resurgence of these devices. Yet, this longing for the past doesn't detract from the excitement for the future. Instead, it informs a more mindful approach to technology, where convenience doesn't trump consideration.

In a way, the evolution from flip phones to smartphones mirrors our society's growth. It reflects our desire for progress, connectivity, and convenience, tempered by a yearning for simplicity and authenticity. As we stand on the cusp of new breakthroughs in mobile technology, such as foldable screens and 5G connectivity, we carry forward the lessons learned from the past.

The interplay between design and functionality, so crucial in the transition from flip phones to smartphones, remains a key consideration as we envision the future of mobile technology. The challenge for designers and engineers is to create devices that not only push the boundaries of what's possible but also remain accessible, intuitive, and, perhaps most importantly, meaningful to users' lives.

As we reflect on this journey, it's clear that the flip phone to smartphone evolution is more than just a chapter in the annals of technology. It's a narrative about aspiration, innovation, and the human experience. It serves as a reminder that in our rapidly changing world, some constants remain—the desire for connection, the joy of discovery, and the endless potential of human creativity.

Embracing the past, therefore, does not mean rejecting the future. On the contrary, it offers a foundation upon which we can build a more thoughtful, inclusive, and sustainable digital age. The flip phone and the smartphone, each in their own way, have contributed to this ongoing story, highlighting the interplay between technology and culture that defines our modern era.

In the context of a 2000s revival, looking back at the evolution from flip phones to smartphones isn't just an exercise in nostalgia. It's an opportunity to gain insights into our relationship with technology, to appreciate how far we've come, and to envisage where we might go next. It reminds us that innovation is not merely about creating new gadgets; it's about envisioning new ways to enhance human life, foster connections, and inspire the world.

The evolution from flip phones to smartphones encapsulates the spirit of the 2000s—a time of rapid change, boundless optimism, and a belief in the power of technology to improve the world. As we navigate the complexities of the 21st century, we would do well to carry these principles forward, guiding us as we shape the future of digital innovation.

The MP3 Revolution: iPods and Portable Music

In the late '90s and early 2000s, the music industry witnessed a seismic shift that forever altered how we interact with our favorite tunes. The advent of MP3 technology and the release of the iPod turned portable music into a personal lifestyle statement, revolutionizing not only the way we consumed music but also how it influenced fashion, social status, and technological innovation. This chapter delves into the heart of this revolution, exploring its origins, impact, and enduring legacy in today's digital age.

Before the iPod, music portability was primarily defined by Walkmans and Discmans, devices that were groundbreaking in their time but limited by physical media. The introduction of MP3 files, however, brought about a groundbreaking change. For the first time, music could be compressed into small files without significant loss of quality, enabling listeners to carry thousands of songs in their pocket. This technological leap was not just about convenience; it signaled a shift towards a more intimate and personalized music experience.

The launch of the iPod in 2001 by Apple, under the visionary leadership of Steve Jobs, was met with skepticism. Critics questioned the device's high price point and the need for such a gadget when cheaper alternatives existed. However, what set the iPod apart was not just its sleek design or user-friendly interface, but the way it integrated with iTunes, offering an unprecedentedly easy way to organize and purchase music. It wasn't long before the iPod became a cultural icon, symbolizing not just taste in music, but a lifestyle choice, a fashion statement, and a badge of tech-savviness.

The impact of the iPod and MP3 technology on the music industry was profound. Record stores and physical albums began their slow march towards obsolescence, replaced by digital downloads. Artists and labels had to adapt to the changing landscape, focusing more on digital sales and finding new ways to engage with fans online. The very structure of music changed, with singles gaining prominence over albums due to the ease of downloading individual songs.

Perhaps the most significant legacy of the MP3 revolution, however, is the democratization of music production and distribution. Aspiring artists no longer needed to rely on record labels to reach their audiences. Instead, they could distribute their music online, directly connecting with fans across the globe. This shift laid the groundwork for the streaming services that dominate the industry today, platforms that owe much of their existence to the trail blazed by early MP3 technology and devices like the iPod.

Yet, despite the rapid evolution of technology, there's a palpable sense of nostalgia for the iPod era. The tactile satisfaction of scrolling through songs with the click wheel, the excitement of meticulously curating playlists, and the joy of sharing music through physical devices hold a special place in the hearts of millennials and early Gen Z'ers. This nostalgia is more than just sentimental; it's part of a broader appreciation for the tangible in an increasingly virtual world.

In recent years, we've seen a resurgence of interest in iPods and other vintage tech, reflecting a desire to reconnect with simpler times. This trend is not merely about reliving the past; it's a reevaluation of what we value in our digital experiences. Attributes like ownership, privacy, and offline access, taken for granted in the era of iPods, are being revisited and reassessed as we grapple with the implications of always-online, cloud-based services.

Moreover, the iPod's influence extends beyond music and technology, touching on aspects of social interaction and personal identity. In its heyday, sharing one's iPod with someone else was a profoundly personal gesture, akin to giving them a window into one's soul. The device's capacity for personalization, from engraved messages to custom playlists, fostered a deep sense of individuality and self-expression.

Education and awareness around digital rights management (DRM) and copyright issues also found a platform during the iPod era. The device played an unwitting role in sparking debates around ownership rights, the ethics of file sharing, and the balance between protecting creators and ensuring consumer access to content. These discussions have shaped policies and attitudes towards digital content that are still relevant today.

As we stand on the threshold of new technological revolutions, the iPod reminds us of the power of technology to transform not just our habits, but our connections, our culture, and our values. It wasn't just a device; it was a gateway to a new way of experiencing music, a harbinger of the digital age, and a testament to the impact of design and innovation on our daily lives.

Reflecting on the iPod era provides us with valuable lessons for the future. It teaches us the importance of designing technology that enhances human experiences without overshadowing them. It reminds us of the value of ownership in an era of streaming and subscriptions. Most importantly, it shows us that even as technology evolves at a breakneck pace, there's enduring power in the personal, tactile, and tangible.

In conclusion, the MP3 revolution, epitomized by the iPod, wasn't just about music. It was about how we relate to technology, to each other, and to the world around us. As we navigate the rapid technological advances of the 21st century, the principles of personalization, usability, and accessibility that the iPod championed remain more relevant than ever. It stands as a beacon of innovation, reminding us that at the heart of every technological leap is the desire to bring us closer to what we love, making our lives richer, more colorful, and infinitely more meaningful.

From AIM to Modern Messaging Apps: The Evolution of Online Communication

The journey from the iconic sounds of America Online's "You've got mail" to the omnipresent "ping" of modern messaging app notifications is more than a story of technological evolution. It's a narrative entwined with the fabric of our social lives, transforming not just how we communicate, but the very essence of our relationships and communities. As we delve into this transition, it's crucial to appreciate the profound impact these platforms have had on identity, connection, and the way we perceive the world around us.

AIM, or AOL Instant Messenger, was more than just a tool; it was a cultural phenomenon that marked the adolescence of many who grew up in the late 90s and early 2000s. The platform was a digital playground, where friendships were forged in the glow of computer screens, away from the watchful eyes of parents. Screen names, away messages, and buddy lists were the digital expressions of our personalities, emotions, and interests. This was a time when online communication began to carve its niche into our social lives, laying the groundwork for the digital-centric world we live in today.

The evolution from AIM to modern messaging apps is a testament to the rapid pace of technological innovation. As smartphones emerged and internet connectivity became ubiquitous, messaging apps evolved to offer more sophisticated features. Platforms like WhatsApp, Facebook Messenger, and WeChat have blurred the lines between texting and social media, making global communication instantaneous and virtually free. This shift has profound implications for our social interactions, enabling connections that span across cities, countries, and continents with ease.

The simplicity and immediacy of modern messaging apps have transformed them into vital tools for both personal and professional communication. They offer an array of features, from video calls and file sharing to stories and stickers, accommodating a myriad of communication preferences and styles. This versatility has made messaging apps indispensable in our daily lives, facilitating a level of connectivity and accessibility that was unimaginable in the AIM era.

However, this evolution in online communication isn't just about technology; it's deeply rooted in the changing dynamics of social interaction and community building. Today's messaging apps are not only platforms for conversation but also spaces for collaboration, learning, and mobilization. They have become ecosystems where communities form over shared interests, social movements gain momentum, and individuals find support and solidarity across distances.

The transition from AIM to modern messaging apps also reflects a shift in our expectations of privacy and security. In the early days of AIM, the concept of data privacy was nascent at best. Today, however, amidst growing concerns over data breaches and surveillance, end-to-end encryption and privacy features have become selling points for messaging apps, reflecting our evolving demands for secure and private communication channels.

Another significant aspect of this evolution is the role of messaging apps in the democratization of information. In the AIM era, information was more centralized, often mediated by news organizations and other gatekeepers. Today, messaging apps facilitate the rapid, peer-to-peer dispersal of information, empowering individuals to share news, mobilize for causes, and challenge narratives in real-time.

The emergence of chatbots and artificial intelligence within messaging apps hints at the future of online communication. These technologies are transforming messaging platforms into interactive spaces that extend beyond human interaction, where individuals can access services, shop, and even control smart home devices. This integration of functionalities suggests that the future of messaging apps lies not just in communication, but in becoming holistic digital platforms that serve multiple aspects of our lives.

Yet, with all these advancements, it's essential to acknowledge the challenges that come with the proliferation of messaging apps. Issues like digital distraction, the erosion of face-to-face communication skills, and the amplification of misinformation are growing concerns. As we navigate this digital landscape, fostering digital literacy and responsible use of technology becomes imperative to ensure that messaging apps enrich rather than detract from our lives.

Reflecting on the journey from AIM to modern messaging apps, it's clear that while the platforms have evolved, the human desire for connection and communication remains constant. These tools have shaped and been shaped by the cultural, social, and technological trends of their times. As we look to the future, the continued evolution of messaging apps will undoubtedly play a pivotal role in shaping our social fabric, influencing not just how we communicate, but how we live, work, and form communities.

In conclusion, the story of online communication's evolution from AIM to modern messaging apps is a microcosm of the broader digital revolution. It encapsulates the incredible pace of technological change and its profound impact on our social interactions. As we reminisce about the sound of a door opening and closing signaling an AIM friend's arrival or departure, we're reminded of the simplicity of the past. Yet, we're propelled forward by the possibilities and potential that modern messaging apps bring to our interconnected world. Embracing this evolution, we continue to forge new paths of connection, understanding, and community in the digital age.

As we embrace the future, let's carry forward the essence of what makes communication meaningful - the desire for genuine connection, understanding, and empathy. In doing so, we ensure that regardless of how technology evolves, our values remain constant, guiding us towards a future where technology enhances, rather than replaces, the richness of human connection.

Thus, the evolution from AIM to modern messaging apps isn't just a chapter in the annals of technology; it's a reminder of our innate need to connect, share, and belong. It's a testament to human ingenuity and adaptability, and a preview of the endless possibilities that await us in the future of online communication. So, as we continue to navigate this ever-changing digital landscape, let's do so with intention, mindfulness, and an unwavering commitment to fostering connections that transcend distance, time, and technology.

Chapter 8:
Beauty and Body Image in the 2000s

The turn of the millennium brought with it a kaleidoscope of beauty standards and ideals that mirrored the era's dynamic blend of optimism and excess. The 2000s were a time when glossy magazines and nascent digital media began dictating trends, forging a period both criticized for its narrow beauty ideals and celebrated for the seeds it sowed towards today's inclusivity. Makeup and hairstyles from this epoch – think glitter eyeshadows, frosted lips, and meticulously straightened tresses – became emblematic of a generation seeking identity in a rapidly changing world. Concurrently, the fitness craze gained momentum, not just through celebrity workout DVDs but as a precursor to today's health-conscious influencers. These aesthetic standards, while seemingly superficial, were underpinned by an evolving conversation around body image that, for better or worse, highlighted the need for diversity and authenticity. This chapter delves into how such beauty and body image trends of the 2000s are being reevaluated and rejuvenated, blending nostalgia with the contemporary push for representation. As we reminisce on the era's iconic looks and societal attitudes, it's crucial to recognize the journey towards today's more inclusive beauty standards. The 2000s, with their mix of high-glam and the burgeoning digital gaze, set the stage for dialogues that challenge and expand our understanding of beauty in a multi-platform, visually driven global culture. This reflective journey isn't just about celebrating or critiquing the past; it's about gleaning insights to inspire a more inclusive, understanding, and compassionate future. Through revisiting the beauty and body image narratives of the 2000s, we can appreciate how far we've come and envision how much further we can go in redefining beauty norms for coming generations.

Makeup and Hairstyles: Glitter and Straight Irons

The early 2000s were a definitive era for both makeup and hairstyles, with trends that were as bold as they were glittery. The makeup of the time was characterized by shimmering eye shadows, frosted lipsticks, and an abundant use of body glitter. This wasn't just about adding a bit of sparkle; it was a statement of self-expression and fun. These looks paired perfectly with the era's iconic hairstyles - sleek, straightened locks achieved with the decade's must-have beauty tool: the straightening iron.

Glitter, in all its forms, became a hallmark of 2000s beauty, finding its way onto eyelids, cheeks, and even sprinkled throughout hair. The philosophy seemed to be 'the more glitter, the better.' This obsession with sparkle wasn't confined to makeup alone. Hair gels and sprays containing glitter allowed teens and young adults to shine literally all over, under the dance floor lights of their favorite clubs or at casual gatherings with friends.

The straightening iron, or flat iron, played a pivotal role in achieving the sleek, pin-straight hair that defined the era's aesthetic. This tool became a staple on every young woman's vanity, transforming wavy and curly locks into smooth, flowing strands. The look was not just about the style itself but the statement it made: a move towards polished, meticulously styled hair that contrasted with the more tousled looks of the previous decade.

Television and music icons of the 2000s heavily influenced these beauty trends. Pop stars and actresses adorned in glittery makeup and impeccably straightened hair became the role models for legions of fans. Their appearances on red carpets, in music videos, and in magazines set the standards for beauty, which millions sought to emulate. The impact of celebrity culture on beauty standards cannot be overstated during this era.

Yet, as with all trends, the fascination with glitter and straightened hairstyles was not merely superficial. It reflected the era's broader cultural currents - a mix of optimism, a yearning for visibility, and a desire for technological innovation. The act of beautifying oneself with glitter and straight hair was, for many, a form of personal expression and empowerment. It was an opportunity to stand out, to be seen, and to be acknowledged.

The explosion of internet culture in the early 2000s also played a significant role in spreading and cementing these beauty trends. Online forums and emerging social media platforms allowed for the exchange of beauty tips and tutorials, making what was once insider knowledge of the beauty industry accessible to all. Teenagers and young adults shared their own experiences and experiments with makeup and hair, creating a vibrant online community united by a shared interest in beauty.

The inclusivity of these trends was also notable. Despite the seeming uniformity of straight hair, individuals of diverse backgrounds found ways to interpret and adapt these styles in ways that suited their personal tastes and cultural identities. This era's beauty trends became a platform for experimentation and a way of challenging traditional norms around beauty and presentation.

As we look back on the 2000s, the era's signature makeup and hairstyles carry a certain nostalgia, encapsulating a period of youth, vibrancy, and change. Yet, they also offer valuable lessons for today's beauty standards. The emphasis on bold, unapologetic self-expression through glitter and sleek hairstyles speaks to a timeless desire to experiment with and redefine beauty norms.

Today, we see a revival of 2000s trends, reinterpreted by a new generation. The return of glitter in makeup and sleek, straightened hairstyles on runways and social media demonstrates the cyclical nature of beauty trends. However, this resurgence is not a mere replication of the past but a reinterpretation that reflects contemporary values of inclusivity, sustainability, and individuality.

This new iteration of 2000s beauty trends is marked by a conscious choice to embrace and adapt retro styles in a way that resonates with today's social and environmental ethos. Glitter, for instance, has seen a shift towards being eco-friendly, with biodegradable options becoming more prevalent. Straightening techniques and tools have also evolved, focusing on hair health and using technology that minimizes damage.

The 2000s beauty trends of glitter and straightened hair remind us of the power of makeup and hairstyling as forms of personal and collective expression. They reflect the dynamic interplay between individual identity and cultural influences, showcasing how beauty standards evolve and adapt over time.

As we navigate the complexities of modern beauty standards, the 2000s offer a beacon of inspiration. They encourage a celebration of uniqueness, a playful approach to beauty, and a reminder that at its core, beauty is an ever-changing, inclusive canvas upon which we can express our most authentic selves.

Ultimately, the legacy of 2000s beauty trends, with its emphasis on glitter and straight irons, is a testament to the era's spirit of innovation, creativity, and individualism. As we look to the future, these trends invite us to reimagine the possibilities of beauty, informed by the past but looking forward to a future where personal expression and inclusivity are at the forefront of beauty culture.

By understanding the impact of these trends and the cultural context in which they emerged, we can appreciate the rich tapestry of influences that continue to shape our concepts of beauty today. The 2000s, with their distinctive makeup and hairstyles, offer a vibrant chapter in the ongoing story of beauty, inviting us all to reflect on our own beauty journeys and the ways in which we choose to define and express ourselves through our appearance.

The Fitness Craze: Celebrity Workout DVDs to Instagram Influencers

The early 2000s witnessed an unprecedented boom in the fitness industry, revolutionizing not just how people worked out, but also how they consumed fitness-related content. This era was marked by the rise of celebrity workout DVDs, a trend that set the stage for the current dominance of Instagram fitness influencers. A fascinating transition that reflects broader changes in technology, celebrity culture, and attitudes towards health and body image.

Celebrity workout DVDs were the hallmark of early 2000s fitness culture. Stars like Jane Fonda, who had initially popularized the trend in the '80s, found new successors in the likes of Carmen Electra and Denise Austin. These videos promised an accessible route to achieving the toned, slim physiques of celebrities, offering a glimpse into seemingly exclusive workout routines. The marketing genius behind these DVDs capitalized on the aspirational desires of their audience, making fitness seem glamorous and attainable all at once.

As technology evolved, so did the medium through which fitness content was delivered. The mid to late 2000s saw a significant shift from physical DVDs to digital content. YouTube became a platform where fitness personalities could upload routines that were accessible to anyone with an internet connection. This democratization of fitness content began to chip away at the monopoly of celebrity-led programs, broadening the fitness landscape.

Simultaneously, the rise of social media platforms, particularly Instagram, further accelerated this shift. Fitness enthusiasts, personal trainers, and even celebrities themselves took to Instagram to post workout clips, healthy eating tips, and motivational content. This platform allowed for a more interactive and engaging form of fitness content, fostering a community of followers who could share tips, progress, and encouragement in real-time.

The appeal of Instagram fitness influencers lies in their perceived authenticity and relatability. They often share their personal journeys, struggles, and successes, making their content more accessible than the untouchable celebrity persona of the early 2000s. This authenticity has contributed significantly to the shift in how fitness is marketed and consumed. It's no longer just about achieving a celebrity body; it's about wellness, mental health, and finding joy in movement.

One of the most noteworthy impacts of this transition is the diversification of fitness ideals. Early 2000s workout DVDs often featured a narrow representation of body types, promoting an often unattainable image of perfection. In contrast, today's fitness influencers cover a broad spectrum of body types, fitness levels, and health goals. This inclusivity has helped shift the narrative from purely aesthetic aspirations to one of overall wellness and body positivity.

This progression mirrors broader cultural trends toward diversity and inclusivity. Body positivity movements have gained momentum alongside the rise of fitness influencers, challenging longstanding beauty standards and encouraging self-acceptance. Fitness content has become a powerful platform for advocacy, with influencers using their reach to promote messages of health at every size, mental wellness, and the importance of self-care.

Moreover, the fitness craze of the 2000s, transitioning into the era of Instagram influencers, demonstrates the changing landscape of celebrity culture. Traditional celebrities, often placed on a pedestal, have given way to 'micro-celebrities' or 'influencers.' These are individuals who may not have traditional fame but wield significant influence within their niche communities. This shift underscores a broader democratization of influence, facilitated by social media platforms that allow anyone to build a following around virtually any topic, including fitness.

The technological advancements of the past two decades have played a pivotal role in this evolution. High-speed internet, smartphones, and the advent of social media platforms have not only changed how fitness content is consumed but also how it's produced. Today, anyone with a smartphone can create and share content, contributing to the ever-expanding universe of fitness information available online.

Despite the overwhelming positives, this new fitness culture is not without its challenges. The same technology that democratizes fitness also facilitates the spread of misinformation. The pressure to maintain a certain image on platforms like Instagram can contribute to unrealistic body standards and negatively impact mental health. Therefore, while celebrating the evolution of fitness culture, it's crucial to approach the content with a critical eye, recognizing the difference between aspirational and attainable health and fitness goals.

Looking forward, the evolution from celebrity workout DVDs to Instagram fitness influencers reveals much about our changing society. It underscores a move towards more inclusive, accessible, and authentic representations of health and fitness. As we navigate the future, it's likely that new technologies and platforms will continue to shape the fitness industry. However, the core desire for connection, authenticity, and well-being will remain a constant driving force behind the ever-evolving landscape of fitness culture.

As our journey from the past into the present shows, the essence of fitness and wellness transcends the medium through which it's delivered. Whether through a DVD player or a smartphone screen, the pursuit of health and happiness remains a universal aspiration. By embracing the lessons of the past and the possibilities of the future, we can continue to build a fitness culture that uplifts, inspires, and includes everyone.

Ultimately, the story of the 2000s fitness craze to today's influencer culture is a testament to the human spirit's adaptability. It reflects our collective quest for improvement, not just in physical form but in mental and emotional wellness. As we look back at the journey thus far, it's clear that while the tools may change, the passion for fitness and the desire for a healthier, happier life continues to burn brightly in the hearts of millions around the globe.

In conclusion, the transformation from celebrity workout DVDs to Instagram influencers marks a significant chapter in the ongoing narrative of fitness and body image. It's a story of progress, shifting paradigms, and the power of community. As we move forward, embracing the changes yet to come, let's carry forward the spirit of inclusivity, authenticity, and wellness that defines the best of what the fitness industry can offer.

Addressing Body Image: Shifts Toward Inclusivity and Diversity

The 2000s era, marked by its glossy magazine covers and runway models with near-impossible standards, set a definitive yet restrictive narrative on beauty and body image. This narrative echoed across the burgeoning digital platforms of the time, bridging the gap between the celebrity world and the everyday reality of its audience. However, as we stride further into the 21st century, a notable shift towards inclusivity and diversity in beauty standards is evident, challenging the monolithic ideals of the past.

Historically, the beauty and fashion industries showcased a narrow spectrum of body types, perpetuating a cycle of exclusivity. This norm was not only unrealistic but also detrimental to the self-esteem of countless individuals who found themselves outside these prescribed ideals. The early 2000s, with their diet culture and size zero craze, amplified these issues, making it a critical period for body image concerns.

In response to this, a movement advocating for body positivity began to gain momentum. This movement, rooted in the principle that all bodies are worthy of acceptance and love, has significantly influenced both the beauty and fashion industries. It's a pushback against the rigid standards that have long dominated these spheres, advocating for a more inclusive representation of beauty that encompasses all sizes, shapes, colors, and abilities.

The rise of social media platforms has played a pivotal role in this shift. Individuals and influencers, wielding the power of hashtags and viral campaigns, have carved out spaces for underrepresented bodies in the digital landscape. Platforms like Instagram, historically critiqued for perpetuating unrealistic beauty standards, have become stages for the body positivity and inclusivity movement. Here, stories of self-love and acceptance unfold daily, challenging societal norms about beauty and body image.

Brands, too, have felt the impact of this cultural shift. Many have taken significant steps towards inclusivity, diversifying their model selection, and expanding their size ranges. This change isn't merely about adding more sizes; it's a rethinking of design philosophy to celebrate diverse body types. It reflects a growing awareness and acceptance that beauty doesn't come in a one-size-fits-all package.

Moreover, the conversation has evolved from body positivity to body neutrality and acceptance. This marks a critical understanding that one's worth isn't tied to their appearance but rather who they are as individuals. It's a healthier, more holistic approach to body image, recognizing that bodies can exist in a state of flux and that's perfectly okay.

Media representation has also seen positive changes. Where once television and films showcased a narrow beauty ideal, now there's a concerted effort to present more diverse and realistic images of people. This shift reflects an understanding of the media's powerful role in shaping societal perceptions of beauty and body image.

Furthermore, the fashion runways, once the bastions of exclusivity, are slowly transforming. Designers who champion inclusivity are gaining recognition, bringing to the forefront models of all sizes, ages, and backgrounds. This change signifies a break from the industry's past, embracing a future where fashion truly is for everyone.

However, it's crucial to note that while strides have been made, the journey towards total inclusivity and diversity in beauty and body image realms is ongoing. Many challenges remain, including overcoming the entrenched attitudes and prejudices that have long governed these industries.

One of the most potent tools in this endeavor has been the vocal advocacy for change. From celebrities using their platforms to speak out against unrealistic beauty standards to everyday individuals sharing their stories of self-acceptance, these voices have been instrumental in driving progress.

Behind this shift is also a growing emphasis on mental health. Recognizing the deep-seated impact of beauty standards on an individual's psychological well-being has been a catalyst for change. It's an acknowledgment that the narratives we craft around beauty and body image carry weight, influencing not just how individuals see themselves but how they navigate the world.

Education plays a key role in sustaining this momentum. By fostering a dialogue from a young age about body diversity, self-acceptance, and the fallacies of comparing oneself to digitally altered images, there's hope for cultivating a more resilient generation, impervious to the toxic beauty standards of the past.

The intersectionality of the body positivity movement has brought to the forefront the need to consider not just body size but also how race, gender, and disability intersect with issues of body image. This comprehensive approach underscores the movement's guiding principle: inclusivity isn't selective. It demands a broad and unyielding embrace of diversity in all its forms.

As this narrative continues to unfold, it's clear that the definition of beauty is undergoing a radical transformation. What was once a narrow, exclusive club is evolving into a vast, welcoming space where diversity is not just accepted but celebrated. This change is more than a trend; it's a movement towards a future where every individual can see their unique beauty reflected back at them, free from the confines of past standards.

In conclusion, the shift towards inclusivity and diversity in addressing body image represents a significant cultural evolution. It's a testament to the collective power of voices demanding change, challenging outdated norms, and reshaping the landscape of beauty and body image for generations to come. It invites us all to be part of this transformative journey, advocating for a world where beauty is as multifaceted and limitless as humanity itself.

Chapter 9:
The Rise, Fall, and Rise of 2000s Reality TV

In a twist of fate as unpredictable as the plotlines of the shows themselves, 2000s reality TV has seen a resurgence that mirrors the very essence of its original appeal. At the dawn of the new millennium, viewers were introduced to a novel form of entertainment that blurred the lines between celebrity and ordinary life, forcing us to question the authenticity of what we saw on screen. Shows like *Survivor* and *The Simple Life* not only captivated audiences with their unscripted drama but also sowed the seeds for a new kind of celebrity culture, one that paved the way for today's influencers. However, as the 2000s progressed, the oversaturation of reality TV led to a decline in its popularity, with many criticizing its impact on societal values and accusing it of cultural degradation.

Just when it seemed like reality TV might be relegated to the annals of entertainment history, a remarkable transformation took place. The very elements that once led to its downfall—the raw emotion, the unfiltered drama, the voyeuristic thrill—have fueled its resurgence. Today's viewers, living in an era dominated by carefully curated social media personas, yearn for a semblance of the authenticity that 2000s reality TV, in all its flawed glory, provided. Moreover, competition shows have evolved, uncovering talents from diverse backgrounds and showcasing stories of perseverance that resonate deeply with a generation championing inclusivity and representation. The impact of 2000s reality TV on today's social media culture is undeniable, with elements of these groundbreaking shows reflected in the way we consume content, engage with influencers, and perceive fame in the digital age.

As we delve into the cyclical nature of entertainment trends, it's clear that 2000s reality TV has left an indelible mark on our collective cultural consciousness. Its rise, fall, and subsequent rise is a testament to our unending search for connection, authenticity, and a mirror to our complex human experiences. As this chapter explores the phenomenon of reality TV's enduring appeal, it serves as a reminder of the power of storytelling, in all its unscripted splendor, to captivate, challenge, and ultimately, unite us.

Survivor to The Simple Life: Reality as Entertainment

In the early 2000s, reality TV underwent a transformation, morphing from a curiosity into a staple of entertainment that dominated television screens worldwide. The era was marked by an unprecedented surge in reality TV shows that ranged from survival competitions to voyeuristic glimpses into the lives of celebrities. The journey from shows like *Survivor* to *The Simple Life* encapsulates this evolution, demonstrating how reality TV became a definitive aspect of early 21st-century pop culture. This phenomenon was not merely about the entertainment on screen; it reflected broader societal shifts and played a pivotal role in shaping the television landscape for years to come.

Survivor, debuting in 2000, was a cultural phenomenon that introduced many viewers to the concept of reality competition. Set in exotic locations, it tested participants' survival skills and strategic acumen, captivating audiences with its blend of adventure, drama, and the unpredictability of human behavior under pressure. Its success paved the way for numerous other competition-based reality shows, each seeking to capture the public's fascination with real people facing extraordinary challenges.

On the flip side, *The Simple Life* offered a different brand of reality entertainment. Premiering in 2003, it showcased socialites Paris Hilton and Nicole Richie as they attempted to live 'ordinary' lives far removed from their privileged backgrounds. The show's humor and sometimes cringe-worthy moments highlighted the cultural gap between the elite and the everyday, simultaneously satirizing and celebrating the absurdities of American life.

The appeal of reality TV in the 2000s lay in its promise of authenticity. Unlike scripted dramas or sitcoms, reality shows purported to offer a glimpse into the unscripted, unrehearsed lives of ordinary and extraordinary people alike. This perceived authenticity, combined with the thrill of competition and the allure of celebrity, made reality TV a compelling proposition for viewers hungry for something new and different.

Technological advancements also played a crucial role in the rise of reality TV. The proliferation of digital video technology made it cheaper and easier to film than ever before, allowing producers to create vast amounts of content at a fraction of the cost of traditional scripted shows. This technological democratization of content creation meant that almost anyone could be a star, blurring the lines between celebrity and obscurity.

The social impact of reality TV during this era cannot be overstated. Shows like *Survivor* and *The Simple Life* not only entertained millions but also sparked conversations about societal values, ethics, and the very nature of reality itself. They questioned what people were willing to do for fame and money, explored the dynamics of social class, and, in some cases, challenged viewers to reconsider their prejudices and assumptions.

Moreover, reality TV was instrumental in shaping the celebrity culture of the 2000s. Participants in these shows, whether they were ordinary people thrust into the spotlight or established stars seeking to show a different side of themselves, became household names. This fame often translated into opportunities in other areas of entertainment, further blurring the lines between traditional celebrity and reality TV stardom.

Additionally, the globalization of television content meant that reality TV formats were not confined to their countries of origin. Shows like *Survivor* were adapted for international audiences, reflecting and reinforcing the global cultural impact of the reality TV phenomenon. This cross-pollination of content contributed to a shared global popular culture, making reality TV a universal language of entertainment.

However, the rise of reality TV was not without its critics. Some accused these shows of dumbing down television and undermining the value of traditional storytelling. Others raised ethical concerns, particularly regarding the treatment of participants and the extent to which reality was manipulated or manufactured by producers. Despite these criticisms, the popularity of reality TV endured, reflecting a cultural appetite for forms of entertainment that felt more immediate and relatable than scripted fare.

In retrospect, the evolution from *Survivor* to *The Simple Life* and beyond represents a critical period in television history. It was a time when the medium experimented with and ultimately embraced the potential of reality as entertainment. As we look back on this era, we can see how it laid the groundwork for the reality TV landscape of today, influencing everything from the types of shows produced to how audiences engage with television content.

As the boundaries between reality and entertainment continue to blur, the legacy of 2000s reality TV is evident in the myriad of reality formats that fill today's streaming and traditional broadcast schedules. From talent competitions to docu-series following influencers and creators, the seeds planted in the early 2000s have blossomed into a diverse garden of content that continues to captivate, amuse, and, occasionally, educate viewers.

The implications of this era extend beyond television. The surge in reality TV coincided with the rise of social media, creating synergies that have transformed how we consume media and perceive reality. Participants and stars of reality shows became influencers, leveraging their television fame to establish presences on platforms like Instagram and YouTube. In turn, these platforms have become staging grounds for the next generation of reality stars, proving the enduring appeal of authentic, unscripted content.

Ultimately, the journey from *Survivor* to *The Simple Life* is a testament to the transformative power of reality TV. It challenged preconceived notions of what television could be, expanded our understanding of celebrity, and reshaped the relationship between audiences and the media they consume. As we explore the resurgence of 2000s trends, it's clear that the legacy of this era's reality TV is not just about nostalgia; it's about recognizing the lasting impact of these pioneering shows on our culture and society.

In a world increasingly dominated by curated feeds and algorithm-driven content, the raw, unvarnished appeal of reality TV reminds us of the value of the unscripted, the unexpected, and the truly real. As we look to the future, it's worth considering how the lessons of the 2000s can inform and inspire the next chapter of reality entertainment, ensuring that it remains as compelling, innovative, and engaging as ever.

Thus, exploring the evolution from *Survivor* to *The Simple Life* is not merely a trip down memory lane. It's an opportunity to reflect on how far we've come and envision where we might go next. In the ever-changing landscape of entertainment, reality TV from the 2000s stands as a bold reminder of television's power to innovate, unite, and inspire.

Competition Shows: Talent Uncovered

The early 2000s marked a distinct era in television history, particularly notable for the meteoric rise of competition-based reality TV shows. Series like *American Idol, America's Next Top Model*, and *Project Runway* took the world by storm, amassing fan bases spanning the globe. What made these shows stand out wasn't just the raw, unfiltered glimpse into the struggles and triumphs of aspiring stars, but the promise that talent, regardless of its background, could be discovered anywhere.

This revolution on the small screen changed public perceptions about fame and success. Suddenly, the path to stardom seemed accessible to the average person with a dream and the courage to pursue it in front of a live audience and panel of judges. This democratization of talent discovery highlighted a shift in cultural values, leaning towards meritocracy and away from nepotism and elitism traditionally associated with the entertainment industry.

Furthermore, these competition shows heralded a new form of entertainment that was both relatable and aspirational. Viewers saw themselves in the contestants' shoes - their hardships, their resilience, and ultimately, their triumphs. The narrative arc of each season, culminating in a rags-to-riches story for the winner, served as a modern-day fairy tale, complete with moral lessons on the value of hard work, perseverance, and believing in one's self.

The judges on these shows became celebrities in their own right, their critiques and praise shaping the trends and tastes of a generation. Figures like Simon Cowell, Tyra Banks, and Tim Gunn became household names, their personal brands intertwined with the success and credibility of the shows themselves.

A crucial aspect of these competition shows was their ability to adapt and evolve. As audiences grew more sophisticated, so too did the formats of these series, incorporating audience voting, social media integration, and behind-the-scenes content. This evolution kept the shows fresh and relevant, ensuring their place in the pantheon of 2000s pop culture.

However, the saturation of the market with numerous spin-offs and similar formats eventually led to a decline in viewership. Audiences began to crave more authentic and less manufactured stories, leading to the rise of different types of reality TV, such as docu-series, which offered a deeper, more nuanced look into the lives and professions of their subjects.

Despite this shift, the impact of 2000s competition shows cannot be overstated. They introduced viewers to diverse talents and stories, broadened the cultural lexicon, and inspired countless individuals to pursue their dreams. The legacy of these shows is evident in the continued popularity of talent competitions, albeit in evolved forms, on both television and online platforms.

The resurgence of interest in these shows among younger generations, courtesy of streaming services and YouTube, underscores their enduring appeal. The themes of aspiration, perseverance, and the transformative power of talent resonate just as strongly with Gen Z as they did with Millennials at the turn of the millennium.

This renewed interest also reflects a nostalgia for the simpler times of the 2000s, before the complexities of today's digital age. In revisiting these shows, viewers find not only entertainment but also a sense of connection to their past selves and the dreams they once harbored.

Moreover, the successes of former contestants in their respective fields serve as a testament to the opportunities these platforms created. Stars like Kelly Clarkson, Jennifer Hudson, and Christian Siriano, who each got their start on such competition shows, have gone on to achieve significant acclaim and influence in their industries.

As we look to the future, the role of competition shows in discovering and nurturing talent remains significant. They've become a key component of the entertainment ecosystem, adapting to changes in culture, technology, and viewer preferences. Their format, which once seemed novel, has now been cemented as a staple of television programming worldwide.

Yet, the essence of these shows—the celebration of talent and the journey towards achieving one's dream—remains unchanged. This enduring theme continues to inspire and captivate audiences, proving that the allure of uncovering new talent is timeless.

In reflecting on the impact of 2000s competition shows, it's clear that their legacy is multifaceted. They've shaped careers, influenced pop culture, and provided countless hours of entertainment. But perhaps most importantly, they've shown us the power of dreams and the limitless potential of human talent.

The return to prominence of these shows highlights not only a nostalgic revival but a reaffirmation of the values they espouse. As a new generation discovers these cultural touchstones, they're reminded that with determination and talent, anything is possible.

As we continue to navigate a rapidly changing cultural and technological landscape, the lessons and legacies of 2000s competition shows serve as a beacon. They remind us that talent, in its many forms, is worth uncovering, celebrating, and supporting. The story of talent discovered is far from over; if anything, it's entering an exciting new chapter.

The Impact of Reality TV on Today's Social Media Culture

Reality TV of the 2000s laid the groundwork for a new era in entertainment, one that seamlessly merged into today's social media culture. Shows like *Survivor* and *The Simple Life* not only captivated millions but also introduced a form of celebrity that was more accessible and seemingly relatable than those from traditional movies and scripted series. This accessibility is something that has been magnified tenfold in the age of social media.

Today, the line between reality TV star and social media influencer is increasingly blurred. Many reality stars have leveraged their television fame to build substantial followings on platforms like Instagram and TikTok, where the essence of reality TV—real people, real reactions, and seemingly unscripted moments—thrives. It's a testament to the staying power of the reality TV formula, now repurposed for the digital age.

The impact of this transition is profound, reshaping not just how celebrities are made, but how they interact with their audience. In the past, fans had to wait for weekly episodes to get a glimpse into the lives of their favorite stars. Now, they can simply open an app and interact with them directly, in real-time. This immediacy has created a more intimate and engaged form of fandom, changing the dynamics of celebrity culture.

Moreover, the very nature of fame has evolved. Reality TV demonstrated that ordinary people could become stars, and social media has taken this idea to new heights. Today, anyone with a smartphone can share their life with the world and potentially rise to fame. Social media platforms have become the new audition room, where original content can catch the eye of millions and catapult creators to stardom.

This democratization of celebrity has its positives, offering a platform for diverse voices and talents who might have been overlooked by traditional media. However, it also raises questions about privacy, the pressure to share more and more personal content, and the impact of constant public scrutiny on individuals' mental health.

Another significant impact of reality TV's influence on social media culture is the concept of "reality" itself. Both mediums play with the idea of authenticity, presenting content that's supposed to be real but is often curated or even manipulated. This blurring of the lines has fostered a skepticism among audiences, making them more discerning consumers of content.

Yet, this hasn't dampened our appetite for reality-based content. On the contrary, there's a growing demand for authenticity, or at least the appearance of it, in both reality TV and social media. Influencers who share not just their successes, but also their struggles, tend to foster a deeper connection with their audience, echoing the appeal of the most successful reality TV shows.

The collaborative potential between reality TV and social media is another area of impact. Many shows now incorporate social media directly into their formats, using it as a tool for audience engagement and even as part of the competition. This synergy has created a more interactive viewing experience, breaking down the fourth wall that traditional TV often maintains.

Moreover, social media has given rise to a form of participatory culture where viewers are not just consumers but also creators. Fans can create their own content inspired by reality TV shows, from memes to fan fiction and commentary videos. This content contributes to the narrative of the show in a very real way, influencing perceptions and even sometimes impacting the direction of the shows themselves.

The educational aspect of this intersection cannot be ignored either. Many influencers and reality stars use their platforms to raise awareness about social issues, much like reality TV has done in the past. This blending of entertainment with education and activism illustrates how the medium can be a force for good, providing visibility for important causes and driving public discourse.

However, the commercialization of both these spaces raises ethical considerations. The push for more content can lead to exploitative practices, with creators feeling pressured to share increasingly personal or sensational aspects of their lives for views. The responsibility of platforms and producers in protecting their stars, many of whom are very young, is a topic of ongoing debate.

The future of reality TV and social media is likely to be even more interconnected. As technology evolves, new platforms and formats will emerge, each offering fresh ways to blur the lines between reality and entertainment. The challenge will be ensuring that these advancements enhance our understanding and appreciation of the human experience, rather than detract from it.

In conclusion, the legacy of 2000s reality TV has significantly shaped today's social media culture, influencing how we view fame, authenticity, and the very nature of entertainment. As we look to the future, it's clear that the principles of reality TV will continue to influence social media, albeit in forms we might not yet be able to imagine. The key will be navigating this landscape with a critical eye, recognizing its potential both to enrich and to complicate our relationship with media.

It's a fascinating time to be a part of this cultural phenomenon, as both creators and consumers. We have the power to shape its evolution, to decide what we value and what we reject. As we engage with reality TV and social media, let's do so thoughtfully, with an awareness of their impact and a commitment to making that impact a positive one.

Through understanding the past, we can influence the future, harnessing the best of what reality TV and social media have to offer. It's a journey worth taking, full of challenges but also opportunities, to create a media landscape that reflects the best of who we are and who we aspire to be.

Chapter 10:
2000s Activism and Social Awareness:
Then and Now

The turn of the millennium heralded a new era not just in technology and entertainment, but also in how we approach activism and social awareness. The 2000s were marked by a burgeoning sense of global interconnectedness, partly thanks to the internet, which dramatically transformed traditional activism. Causes like the Green Movement and early environmental advocacy campaigns showed us the power of collective action, often organized through burgeoning online platforms. This period also saw a significant shift towards social justice, moving from awareness campaigns to the nascent stages of hashtag activism, a trend that would explode in the following decade.

Now, we're witnessing a fascinating evolution of 2000s activism reinterpreted by a new generation. Today's movements are built on the foundation laid by their predecessors but have expanded in scope and sophistication, leveraging social media's omnipresence to mobilize, educate, and effect change at unprecedented speeds. The influence of 2000s activism on modern movements is undeniable, as we see the seeds sown during the early days of the internet blossom into the dynamic landscape of digital activism we navigate today. This chapter dives into the heart of 2000s activism, tracing its development and examining its lasting impact on how we fight for a better world. It's a journey through the evolution of social awareness, from grassroots email campaigns to the viral power of hashtags, exploring how these early 21st-century movements have shaped our current landscape of global activism.

The Green Movement: Early Environmental Advocacy

At the dawn of the 21st century, environmentalism was not the widespread concern it is today. The early 2000s marked a pivotal era where the seeds of what we now recognize as the green movement were sown. This period set the stage for a transformative wave of environmental advocacy, driven by a mixture of grassroots activism, scientific research making headlines, and a growing awareness of the planet's fragility. It wasn't just about saving the rainforests or recycling anymore; it was about fundamentally altering the way society interacted with the natural world.

During this time, the discourse around climate change began to shift. Scientists were becoming increasingly vocal about the imminent dangers posed by global warming, with the Intergovernmental Panel on Climate Change (IPCC) reports gaining public attention. The alarming evidence presented in these documents helped to catalyze a movement that was ready to challenge industrial giants and push for policy change at both national and international levels.

One of the most influential moments of early environmental advocacy was the release of Al Gore's documentary, "An Inconvenient Truth," in 2006. The film brought the realities of climate change into the living rooms of ordinary people around the world. It was a wakeup call for many, transforming public perception from skepticism into a more urgent acknowledgment of the environmental crises facing the planet.

But the movement wasn't just happening on the screens or in the papers; it was taking shape on the streets. Grassroots organizations began to proliferate, mobilizing communities to take action. Whether it was through local clean-up initiatives, tree planting events, or protests against polluting industries, people were starting to make their voices heard. It was a time of awakening, of recognizing that change starts with individual and collective action.

Moreover, the early 2000s saw the rise of sustainable living as a popular lifestyle choice. Farmers' markets, organic food, and eco-friendly products started to become more mainstream, endorsed by celebrities and supported by a growing number of consumers who wanted to make ethical and environmentally sound choices. This shift also brought attention to the concept of "reduce, reuse, recycle," encouraging people to rethink their consumption habits.

In the realm of politics and policy, environmental advocacy led to some significant milestones. The Kyoto Protocol, an international treaty that committed its parties to reduce greenhouse gas emissions, came into force in 2005. Although not without its criticisms and challenges, the protocol represented an important step forward in global efforts to address climate change. It showed that environmental issues were beginning to take center stage in international diplomacy.

Apart from global initiatives, local governments and cities began adopting greener policies, from improving public transport and cycling infrastructure to investing in renewable energy sources. These changes demonstrated that environmental advocacy was capable of influencing policy at multiple levels, driving a gradual but tangible shift towards sustainability.

Education also played a crucial role in early environmental advocacy. Schools and universities started integrating environmental science and sustainability into their curricula, empowering younger generations with the knowledge and passion to protect their planet. These educational efforts aimed to cultivate a culture of responsibility and action among the youth, ensuring that the movement would continue to grow and evolve.

However, the journey was not without its challenges. Environmental advocates often faced opposition from industries reliant on fossil fuels and from political figures skeptical of climate change. Yet, despite these hurdles, the movement pressed on, fueled by the conviction that the wellbeing of the planet and future generations was at stake.

The legacy of early 2000s environmental advocacy is immense. It laid the groundwork for the vibrant, diverse, and global green movement we see today. From the Paris Agreement to the rise of youth-led movements like Fridays for Future, the roots can be traced back to the efforts of those who, two decades ago, refused to stay silent.

Looking back, the early 2000s were a time of awakening and action, where the seeds of environmental consciousness were planted in the fertile ground of a society ready for change. The green movement of that era taught us invaluable lessons about perseverance, the power of collective action, and the importance of safeguarding our planet for future generations.

As we face the environmental challenges of our current times, the story of early environmental advocacy serves as a poignant reminder that change is possible, and that each of us has a role to play in making the world a greener, more sustainable place. It's a call to action, inspiring us to carry forward the momentum with the same spirit of determination and hope that defined the green movement of the 2000s.

In reflecting on the early days of environmental advocacy, we're reminded that the fight for a sustainable planet is an ongoing one. The achievements and setbacks of the past inform our path forward, offering lessons in resilience, innovation, and the unyielding belief that a better world is within our reach. As we continue to navigate the challenges of climate change and environmental degradation, the legacy of the 2000s green movement serves as both a foundation and a beacon, guiding us towards a future where harmony with nature isn't just an ideal, but a reality.

Ultimately, the early environmental advocacy of the 2000s reminds us of the power of informed action and passionate commitment to a cause. It stands as a testament to what can be achieved when we come together, armed with knowledge and driven by the desire to protect and preserve our planet. As we look back, we're not just commemorating a movement; we're reinvigorating our resolve to continue the vital work of those who paved the way, ensuring that their legacy lives on in our ongoing efforts to make the world a better place for all its inhabitants.

The 2000s were more than just a decade; they were a turning point in our collective environmental consciousness. As we forge ahead, let's carry with us the lessons learned, the progress made, and the unwavering spirit of early environmental advocacy. In doing so, we honor the past and embrace a future where sustainability and respect for the Earth are at the heart of all we do.

Social Justice: From Awareness Campaigns to Hashtag Activism

The turn of the millennium was not just a pivotal moment in technology and fashion; it also ushered in a new era of social justice activism. As we look back on the 2000s, it's clear that the methods and approaches to activism underwent significant transformations, adapting to the digital revolution that was unfolding. This evolution from traditional awareness campaigns to the dynamic realm of hashtag activism has reshaped the landscape of social justice, making it more accessible and immediate than ever before.

At the heart of early 2000s activism was the growing awareness of global issues, from environmental campaigns to the fight for human rights. Organizations and activists harnessed the power of burgeoning internet platforms to reach wider audiences, sharing information and rallying support through websites and forums. Campaigns like the Live 8 concerts in 2005 demonstrated the potent combination of celebrity endorsement and global media to shine a light on the G8 countries' policies affecting Africa, merging entertainment with advocacy in unprecedented ways.

However, as impactful as these campaigns were, they often required significant resources and platforms to break into mainstream consciousness. Not everyone had the means or opportunity to participate in large-scale protests or high-profile events, limiting the scope of who could engage with these critical social issues. This is where the leap to digital platforms, notably through the rise of social media, began to democratize social justice activism.

The introduction of platforms like Twitter, Facebook, and Instagram opened new avenues for activism. Suddenly, it wasn't just about having access to physical spaces or resources; having a social media account became enough to participate in global conversations. The Arab Spring in the early 2010s exemplified this shift, showing the world the power of social media to mobilize, inform, and create communities of resistance across borders.

Hashtag activism became a key player in this new age of advocacy. #BlackLivesMatter, born out of response to the acquittal of Trayvon Martin's murderer in 2013, transcended its origins to become a global movement against systemic racism and police brutality. Such hashtags do more than just trend; they create spaces for stories and experiences to be shared, for solidarity to be formed, and for issues to be pushed into the public eye.

Yet, with the rise of hashtag activism, criticism has followed. Detractors argue that it encourages "slacktivism," a way for individuals to feel they've contributed to a cause with minimal effort, without effecting real change. While it's valid to question the tangible outcomes of online activism, it's undeniable that these digital movements have succeeded in raising awareness and fostering communities that might not have otherwise engaged with these issues.

The beauty of social media lies in its ability to amplify marginalized voices. Campaigns like #MeToo, initially started in 2006 but gaining viral momentum in 2017, demonstrated the platform's power to break silences around sexual assault and harassment, holding powerful individuals accountable. Social media has given those who historically had been sidelined from mainstream activism a chance to lead and frame their narratives on their own terms.

Moreover, the digital era of activism has introduced innovative methods of organizing and protesting. Virtual protests, online petitions, and crowdfunding for bail funds and legal fees have become standard tools in an activist's arsenal, enabling swift, coordinated responses to injustices. These tools not only broaden participation but also ensure that activism can continue even amidst challenges like a global pandemic.

As we look towards the future, the intersection of technology and activism promises even more possibilities. Artificial intelligence, virtual reality, and decentralized blockchain platforms offer new ways to engage with and fight for social justice. However, as technology evolves, so too will the strategies of those opposing progress. The digital divide remains a significant barrier, reminding us that access to the internet is still a privilege not afforded to all.

The journey from awareness campaigns to hashtag activism encapsulates the evolution of social justice in the digital age. As we reflect on these changes, it's crucial to remember that at the core of all activism—digital or otherwise—is the desire for a more equitable and just world. The methods may have transformed, but the goal remains the same. It's up to us, the inheritors of this legacy, to continue the fight, leveraging the tools and platforms at our disposal to make lasting change.

In navigating the complexities of modern activism, it's essential to stay informed, critical, and supportive of movements that align with the principles of justice and equity. Social media has given us the power to spread information and mobilize at an unprecedented scale. Yet, this power comes with responsibility—to verify the information we share, to listen to the voices of those directly affected, and to move beyond the digital realm into tangible, real-world support and action.

The progression from traditional campaign strategies to the nuanced world of digital activism is not merely a shift in tactics but a broadening of the democratic process. It's a testament to human creativity and resilience, a reflection of our collective desire to seek out justice, even when faced with seemingly insurmountable odds. As we continue to navigate the challenges and opportunities of activism in the digital age, let's do so with the knowledge that every tweet, every post, and every hashtag is a step towards building the world we wish to see.

In embracing the lessons from the past and the potential of the future, the journey of social justice from awareness campaigns to hashtag activism illustrates a rich tapestry of human engagement with the world's sufferings and injustices. This evolution offers hope and a call to action for everyone, reminding us that change is possible, and it often starts with a single post, a single hashtag, a single voice demanding to be heard. Let's carry forward the legacy of the 2000s into the next decade with courage, compassion, and an unwavering commitment to justice.

The Influence of 2000s Activism on Modern Movements

The activism of the 2000s, characterized by its vibrancy and its burgeoning digital platform use, has undeniably left an indelible mark on modern movements. This era introduced a new lexicon of social justice and environmental consciousness that has been expanded and redefined by subsequent generations. As we delve into this transformation, it's crucial to understand the roots from which today's activism has sprouted.

At the turn of the millennium, the global community faced a new set of challenges and opportunities. The advent of the internet and mobile communication transformed the way activists organized and spread their messages. Campaigns that once relied on physical pamphlets and word-of-mouth could now reach a global audience with the click of a button. This digital evolution in the 2000s laid the groundwork for the viral social justice movements we see today.

One of the most prominent features of 2000s activism was its commitment to environmental concerns, predating the widespread acknowledgment of climate change seen in today's discourse. This period saw the inception of movements like the Green Belt Movement, which, while founded in the late 20th century, gained significant international recognition in the 2000s, influencing modern environmental advocacy groups.

Similarly, social justice campaigns in the 2000s began addressing issues ranging from global poverty to AIDS awareness, setting the stage for the hashtag activism prevalent in current movements. These early initiatives democratized activism, showing that one didn't need to be part of a large organization to effect change. Instead, individuals armed with a cause and a connection could mobilize masses.

Modern movements owe a debt to the 2000s approach to grassroots organizing. The techniques developed during this era, such as using social media to organize protests or crowdfunding campaigns for social causes, are now standard. This period proved that activism could adapt and thrive alongside technological advancements, a lesson that continues to inspire today's organizers.

The global protests against the Iraq War in the early 2000s, for instance, showcased the potential for transnational solidarity and set a precedent for international cooperation among activist groups. This spirit of global interconnectedness persists in contemporary movements like the Fridays for Future climate strikes, which draw participants from around the world.

Moreover, the 2000s were marked by a significant push for diversity and inclusion, with activists challenging mainstream narratives and advocating for representation across different sectors. This pursuit has only intensified, as current movements continue to highlight issues related to race, gender, and sexuality, building on the foundational work of their predecessors.

The DIY ethos of the 2000s, fueled by the rise of blogs and independent media, has also influenced modern activism. Today, we see a continuation of this trend, with platforms like Instagram and TikTok serving as spaces for advocacy and education, enabling individuals to share stories and galvanize support on a scale previously unimaginable.

Education campaigns of the 2000s, which often made use of emerging online platforms to disseminate information, paved the way for the informative and educational content that floods social media channels today. These early initiatives demonstrated the power of knowledge sharing as a form of activism, a principle that remains pertinent.

The anti-globalization movements of the 2000s, characterized by their critique of capitalism and neocolonialism, have evolved into today's broader discussions around economic equity and justice. The Occupy Wall Street movement, for instance, can trace its ideological roots back to the protests and debates of the early 2000s.

It's also pivotal to recognize the transformation in how activists communicate and organize. The 2000s were a testing ground for what is possible when technology and passion intersect. The effective use of online forums and communication tools from that era has informed the multifaceted digital strategies employed by movements today.

The focus on youth participation during the 2000s has carried over into current activism, with young people now at the forefront of various movements. This generational shift has brought fresh perspectives and renewed vigor to long-standing issues, proving the enduring influence of the activism from the 2000s.

However, it's not just about the tactics and platforms; it's also about the ethos. The 2000s instilled a sense of hope and the belief that collective action could lead to meaningful change. This optimism is a thread that connects past and present movements, inspiring a new wave of activists to push boundaries and envision a more equitable world.

In reflecting on the legacy of 2000s activism, it's evident that its impact extends far beyond specific campaigns or technologies. It's a mindset, a methodology, and a moral compass that continues to guide the actions and aspirations of those seeking to make a difference. As we look to the future, the lessons and legacies of the 2000s activism remain a beacon for navigating the complex social and environmental challenges of our time.

In conclusion, the activism of the 2000s has profoundly shaped the landscape of modern movements. Its innovative use of digital tools, commitment to inclusivity, and emphasis on grassroots organizing have become hallmarks of contemporary activism. As we move forward, harnessing the spirit and strategies of the 2000s will be crucial in creating a more just and sustainable world. The decade's activism has not only influenced the trajectory of social movements but has also empowered a new generation to carry forward the torch of change, illustrating the timeless nature of its impact.

Chapter 11:
The Internet Culture: Memes, Virality, and Web Communities

In the labyrinth of the early 2000s internet culture, memes became the secret handshake of digital natives, virality the coveted elixir of content creators, and web communities the sanctuaries for souls scattered across the globe. This era heralded the democratization of content creation, where anyone with an internet connection could contribute to the sprawling tapestry of web culture. Memes evolved from simple humorous images to complex signifiers of societal moods, embodying the zeitgeist with a precision no traditional media could achieve. The phenomenon of virality, meanwhile, transformed obscure content into overnight sensations, demonstrating the internet's unpredictable power in shaping public discourse. Within this digital ecosystem, niche web communities flourished, offering havens for shared interests and identities. These early forums and social networks laid the groundwork for today's vibrant online culture, highlighting the enduring human need for connection, expression, and laughter. Through exploring the roots and repercussions of these elements, we uncover not just the mechanics of internet culture, but the heart of a generation ready to navigate the crossroads of nostalgia and innovation, threading the past through the eye of the future.

The Birth of Memes: Impact on Communication

The story of internet culture can't be told without a deep dive into the world of memes. These simple yet ingenious creations have woven themselves into the very fabric of online and offline conversation, altering the way we communicate, share ideas, and even how we relate to one another. The emergence of memes in the early days of the internet marked a significant shift in digital expression, one that would forever change the landscape of online interaction.

Memes, in essence, are ideas, behaviors, or style that spread from person to person within a culture. Initially, they were just humorous images, videos, or text that were shared and modified slightly by each user. However, as they evolved, so did their uses and implications, morphing into a language of their own. Their ability to convey complex ideas and emotions succinctly made them an instant hit across web forums and burgeoning social media platforms.

The role of memes in shaping online culture can't be understated. They became the currency of the internet, a way to participate in a larger conversation without needing an elaborate setup or context. This accessibility opened up new avenues for people to express themselves, creating a democratic space where anyone's idea could potentially become the next big sensation. It was a manifestation of the internet's promise of democratized content creation and consumption.

As memes permeated deeper into our daily lives, their impact on communication became more profound. They started as a means to entertain and connect with like-minded individuals but soon became a tool for social commentary, political satire, and a platform for raising awareness about various issues. This shift from purely entertainment to a mixed bag of purposes showcases the versatility and power of memes as a form of expression.

The linguistic metamorphosis brought about by memes is particularly noteworthy. Phrases from popular memes have entered our daily vernacular, demonstrating the seamless integration of internet culture into real-world interactions. This crossover has led to the creation of a hybrid language, one that's equally understood across different cultures and geographical barriers, thanks in part to the universal appeal of humor and relatability found in memes.

However, the journey of memes has not been without its challenges. As much as they bring joy and foster community, they have also been weaponized for spreading misinformation and creating divisiveness. The ease with which memes can be created and shared has posed unique challenges in combating the spread of false information, proving that with great power comes great responsibility.

The educational potential of memes is an area that's gaining attention. Teachers and educators are increasingly incorporating memes into their instruction, leveraging their engaging nature to connect with students on a cultural level. This approach not only makes learning more enjoyable but also demonstrates the evolving landscape of educational tools, where pop culture and academia intersect in creative ways.

Memes have also significantly impacted marketing and advertising strategies. Brands that have successfully tapped into meme culture often enjoy higher engagement rates, as they're perceived as more relatable and in tune with current trends. This shift marks a departure from traditional advertising, highlighting the importance of adaptability and cultural awareness in today's fast-paced world.

The international reach of memes underscores the global village concept, illustrating how ideas can traverse continents in seconds, fostering a sense of global community. This universal language of memes has bridged cultural gaps, proving that humor and relatability are not bound by geographical locations.

Despite their ubiquity, the question of copyright and originality in meme culture remains a contentious issue. The collaborative and iterative nature of meme creation challenges traditional notions of ownership and intellectual property, sparking debates about creativity, sharing, and copyright in the digital age.

Looking to the future, the evolution of memes promises to be as dynamic as their history. With advances in technology, particularly in AI and machine learning, the way we create, share, and interact with memes is bound to change. These changes will likely bring about new forms of memes that we can scarcely imagine today, further altering the landscape of digital communication.

The impact of memes on communication is a testament to the human capacity for creativity and adaptation. They've evolved from simple internet jokes to a complex language that transcends borders, cultures, and mediums. As we look back on the birth and rise of memes, it's clear they are more than just a passing internet trend. They are a pivotal part of our digital lexicon, continually shaping and reflecting the zeitgeist of our times.

As we delve further into the 21st century, the legacy of memes in shaping internet culture and communication is undeniable. They serve as a reminder of the internet's power to bring people together, to create a shared sense of identity and community among disparate groups. In a world that's increasingly digital, memes stand out as a beacon of collective creativity and a mirror to our society's values, fears, and aspirations.

In conclusion, the birth of memes and their ensuing impact on communication showcases a fascinating journey of digital culture. From their humble beginnings to their current status as a cultural phenomenon, memes have not only changed the way we communicate but have also altered our perception of what it means to be part of a global community. As we move forward, it's clear that memes will continue to be an integral part of our digital and real-world interactions, constantly evolving with the times while remaining a relatable and uniting force.

Viral Trends and Challenges: The Double-Edged Sword

Viral trends and challenges have encased themselves in the fabric of internet culture like the threads of a vast, ever-expanding tapestry. They are the moments that define the zeitgeist, encapsulating the essence of creativity, spontaneity, and, at times, the reckless abandon of the digital era. As much as they have brought laughter, unity, and awareness to various causes, they've also shown the capacity for harm, misinformation, and unintended consequences.

The allure of virality is undeniable. Who among us hasn't been tempted to join in on the latest challenge or share a meme that perfectly encapsulates our thoughts and feelings? These trends are more than just fleeting moments; they are a testament to the power of communal experience in the digital age. They transcend geographic and cultural boundaries, uniting us in shared amusement, empathy, or even outrage.

Yet, for all the joy and community they can bring, viral trends and challenges tread a fine line between harmless fun and potential danger. The quest for likes, shares, and fleeting internet fame can drive individuals to push boundaries in ways that can lead to physical harm or emotional distress. From the innocuous to the downright hazardous, challenges have evolved, mirroring the complexities of the online world itself.

Consider the Ice Bucket Challenge, a phenomenon that swept the internet and did so much more than give viewers a chuckle at the expense of friends drenched in ice-cold water. It raised unprecedented awareness and funds for amyotrophic lateral sclerosis (ALS), demonstrating the potential for viral trends to catalyze positive social change. However, not all challenges yield such beneficial outcomes, with some leading to injuries or exposing participants to ridicule and cyberbullying.

The rapid pace of the internet means that today's viral sensation is tomorrow's forgotten meme. This ephemeral nature beckons us to question the lasting impact of these trends beyond the instant gratification they offer. As we participate and share, it's essential to reflect on the implications of our digital footprints. How do these trends shape public discourse, influence behavior, and affect mental health?

In the quest for virality, the line between entertainment and exploitation can blur. Reality TV stars, social media influencers, and ordinary individuals alike have all found their lives and actions under the microscope, dissected by the court of public opinion. The pressure to maintain relevance and engage audiences can lead to questionable judgment, where the desire to captivate overshadows the responsibility to convey authenticity and maintain ethical standards.

Yet, the phenomenon of virality is not without its virtues. It has democratized fame, enabling voices from the margins to be heard on a global stage. Undiscovered talents find audiences beyond their wildest dreams, social movements gain momentum, and communities of support form around shared experiences and interests. These are the moments when the internet reveals its true potential to connect and uplift.

As digital citizens, our engagement with viral trends and challenges wields power. With every click, share, and participate, we contribute to the shaping of the online narrative. This engagement carries a responsibility to discern the content we amplify from fleeting trends to those that inspire meaningful action and contribute to the greater good.

The dichotomy of viral trends as both a force for good and a potential catalyst for harm underscores the complexity of our digital lives. It's a reminder that, amidst the rush to partake in the next big thing, we must navigate the online world with critical awareness and empathy. By doing so, we can embrace the positive aspects of viral culture while mitigating its risks.

The phenomena of trends and challenges, while emblematic of the internet's capacity to unite and entertain, also serve as a mirror reflecting society's values, concerns, and aspirations. As we look forward, it's clear that these viral moments will continue to play a significant role in our digital lexicon, evolving with the platform and the people that propel them.

The resilience of internet culture, with its memes, virality, and communities, lies in its adaptability. It evolves, sometimes unpredictably, mirroring the shifts in societal norms and technological advancements. This dynamism challenges us to keep pace, to understand its flow, and to harness its power responsibly.

In navigating the landscape of viral challenges and trends, we find a microcosm of the larger digital experience — one fraught with pitfalls but also abundant in opportunities for connection, understanding, and positive change. It's a testament to the human desire to share experiences, to participate in the collective consciousness, and to make our mark, however fleeting it may be.

The discussion on viral trends and challenges, thus, is more than an exploration of the phenomena themselves; it's a conversation about us — our hopes, our fears, and our need to connect. As we delve into the impacts and implications of these trends, we uncover layers of our collective psyche, our digital ethos, and perhaps, our path forward in this interconnected world.

In closing, the dance between the allure of virality and the responsibility it entails is ongoing. As members of an ever-evolving digital society, our role in shaping its direction is crucial. By fostering an environment where creativity and empathy coexist, we can ensure that the legacy of our viral moments is one of positive impact and shared joy.

So, as we scroll, share, and participate in the next viral trend, let's do so with awareness and intention, mindful of the immense power we hold at our fingertips — the power to influence, to change, and to connect in ways that enrich not just our own lives but the tapestry of the digital age itself.

Niche Communities and the Early Forums: Finding a Tribe Online

The turn of the millennium heralded not just a new era in technology and fashion, but also in how we connected with each other. As we ventured into the 2000s, the internet began to evolve from a burgeoning network of information to a vibrant ecosystem teeming with niche communities and early forums. It was here, in these digital enclaves, where many found a tribe online, a concept that was revolutionary at a time when mainstream culture often felt exclusionary.

Before Twitter threads and Instagram stories, early internet forums served as the epicenters of online culture. Platforms like LiveJournal, and later, Reddit, allowed individuals to create, share, and discuss within communities that shared their specific interests or experiences. Whether it was a forum dedicated to a particular band, a nascent form of what would later be known as fandoms, or online bulletin boards for technology aficionados, these spaces provided a haven for passionate discourse.

Interestingly, what made these early forums so special was their relative obscurity. In an age before viral content and social media algorithms, finding a forum that catered to your specific niche felt like uncovering a hidden gem. It was a digital rite of passage that fostered a sense of belonging and identity among its members.

The beauty of these online communities lay not just in their content, but in the interactions they facilitated. Long before 'community management' became a profession, early forum moderators and members organically developed norms and etiquettes that shaped the culture of these spaces. This self-regulation helped maintain a respectful and engaging environment where ideas could flourish.

It's crucial to understand that these communities were more than just spaces for leisure or fandom. They were critical in fostering a sense of identity for people who often felt marginalized or misunderstood in their offline lives. For LGBTQ+ individuals, people with disabilities, or those with niche hobbies, forums offered a sense of visibility and representation that was rare in mainstream media at the time.

One can't discuss the impact of early online forums without acknowledging the role they played in music and pop culture. Sites like Napster not only transformed how we accessed music but also how fans connected with each other and supported their favorite artists. It was an early glimpse into how the internet would later enable artists to break the traditional barriers of the music industry.

Similarly, the gaming community found a strong foothold in early online forums, shaping not just the culture around video games but also influencing their development. Forums allowed gamers to share tips, organize multiplayer sessions, and even contribute to game development through beta testing feedback, a precursor to today's widespread fan involvement in the industry.

Yet, these forums were not without their challenges. Issues of privacy, security, and cyberbullying were as pertinent then as they are today. However, the collective effort to create safe and inclusive spaces often led to pioneering approaches to digital community management.

As the 2000s progressed, these niche communities began to evolve. The advent of social media platforms like MySpace, and later Facebook and Twitter, changed how we interacted online. While forums still existed, the immediacy and visual nature of these new platforms began to overshadow the text-heavy forum posts. However, the foundations laid by these early communities — a sense of belonging, the importance of niche interests, and the power of collective identity — continued to influence digital culture.

It's fascinating to see how today's online communities bear the imprints of these early forms of digital congregation. Subreddits, Facebook groups, and niche Twitter threads all owe a debt to the forum culture of the 2000s. Even as platforms evolve, the human desire for connection and community remains a constant.

The resurgence of interest in 2000s culture among Gen Z and millennials isn't just a matter of nostalgia. It's a testament to the enduring impact of that era's approach to community building. These early digital spaces demonstrated that technology could bring us together in ways that were once unimaginable, setting the stage for the social media landscape of today.

In many ways, the legacy of early forums is a reminder of the internet's potential to create meaningful connections. In a time when online discourse often seems divided, looking back at these communities shows us the importance of finding common ground and celebrating niche interests.

As we look to the future, the evolution of digital communities holds infinite possibilities. By examining the past, we can envision a digital landscape that values inclusivity, provides a platform for all voices, and continues to bring people together over shared passions. The early forums of the 2000s taught us that online, everyone can find their tribe.

So, as we navigate the ever-changing terrain of the internet, let us carry forward the spirit of those early forums. Building communities that thrive on respect, enrich our lives, and remind us that, in the vast expanse of the digital universe, there's a place for everyone. The journey of finding a tribe online is ongoing, and its legacy is ours to shape for the generations to come.

Chapter 12:
The Future of the 2000s: What Comes Next?

The allure of the 2000s isn't just a passing fad; it's a dynamic reflection of our continuous journey through cultural reevaluation, begging us to question what indeed comes next in this cyclical dance of nostalgia and innovation. As we stand at this unique crossroads, the intersection of sustainability breathes new life into our beloved 2000s trends, crafting a future where eco-conscious decisions meld seamlessly with the aesthetics of an era we're not ready to let go of. This green twist isn't just about recycling old ideas but reinvigorating them, underscoring the importance of our planet alongside our passion for past trends. Furthermore, the unfolding narrative of the 2000s revival isn't one to be written by a single generation. Gen Z, alongside millennials, are not merely bridging a gap but are constructing a robust, shared cultural bridge that spans wide, embracing the past while keenly influencing the future. Through this unique partnership, we're poised to witness the resurrection of 2000s culture, not as it was but as what it could be—drenched in diverse voices, sustainable practices, and an undying zeal for innovation. So, as we dive into this chapter, let's explore how the reinterpreted threads of the early aughts could weave the fabric of our shared future, driven by the relentless spirit of those ready to carry forward the torch of cultural renaissance.

Sustainability: Reinterpreting 2000s Trends with a Green Twist

As we delve into the future of the 2000s, embracing the past doesn't mean we can't evolve. The resurrection of 2000s trends offers us a unique opportunity to stitch sustainability into the fabric of our cultural revival. This chapter explores how the zeitgeist of the 2000s is being reimagined through a greener lens, intertwining nostalgia with the urgent need for environmental consciousness.

During the original 2000s era, fast fashion began its rapid ascent, propelled by the desire for quick, affordable updates to personal style. Today, we're reevaluating this approach, recognizing the heavy toll it takes on our planet. As low-rise jeans, cargo pants, and velour tracksuits make their comeback, ethical production and sustainable materials have come to the forefront. Businesses are innovating with recycled fabrics and more efficient manufacturing processes, ensuring that our love for Y2K fashion leaves a lighter footprint.

Similarly, the beauty industry of the 2000s, known for its glittery, maximalist aesthetic, is undergoing a transformation. Modern consumers prioritize products that are cruelty-free, made with natural ingredients, and housed in eco-friendly packaging. The shift towards sustainability doesn't mean sacrificing the playful spirit of 2000s beauty; instead, it elevates it, allowing us to celebrate self-expression in a way that's conscientious and respectful to our environment.

Technology, a defining feature of the 2000s, also finds itself at the intersection of nostalgia and innovation. Gadgets that defined the decade, such as flip phones and MP3 players, are being revisited with sustainability in mind. Efforts to reduce e-waste through recycling programs and the development of more energy-efficient devices reflect a commitment to merging 2000s tech enthusiasm with today's environmental priorities.

The 2000s were also marked by the beginnings of the digital revolution, changing the way we communicate and consume media. In our current era, the focus is on digital sustainability, optimizing online spaces to reduce their carbon footprint. This includes more efficient data storage solutions and advocating for responsible digital consumption habits, ensuring that our internet use supports a healthier planet.

Music and media from the 2000s are finding new life through sustainable practices as well. The resurgence of vinyl records, viewed through a sustainable lens, encourages the use of recycled materials and more eco-friendly production methods. Streaming services, too, are exploring ways to minimize their environmental impact, making our nostalgia-driven media binges a bit greener.

One of the most vibrant aspects of 2000s culture was its activism, particularly regarding environmental issues. Today, we're building on that legacy, pushing for more significant action against climate change and promoting sustainable living. Social media, a tool that came of age during the 2000s, now serves as a powerful platform for environmental advocacy, demonstrating how past and present can unite for a cause.

Outdoor and lifestyle brands that gained popularity in the 2000s, known for their rugged, adventurous aesthetic, are leading by example in sustainability. Companies are revisiting their classic products, reengineering them with sustainable materials and ethical production methods, proving that durability and environmental responsibility can go hand in hand.

The food industry, too, reflects this shift towards sustainability, with 2000s favorites like organic food and vegetarian diets gaining even more traction today. This turn towards more sustainable eating habits not only benefits our health but also supports agricultural practices that are kinder to the Earth.

In the realm of transportation, the 2000s brought us the rise of hybrid cars, a landmark step towards sustainable living. Now, we're witnessing the evolution of this concept with the proliferation of electric vehicles, bike-sharing programs, and a renewed interest in public transport, reshaping our mobility to be more in harmony with the planet.

Interior design trends from the 2000s, characterized by minimalism and tech-inspired aesthetics, are being reinterpreted with sustainability in mind. Furniture and home decor are increasingly made from recycled or responsibly sourced materials, blending style with environmental mindfulness.

Even in the area of entertainment and leisure, sustainability is making its mark. Movie studios and television production companies are implementing green practices, from reducing plastic use on set to embracing digital script management, ensuring that our favorite 2000s revivals are produced in an eco-friendly manner.

As we relive the excitement of the 2000s, incorporating a green twist doesn't just make sense—it's a necessity. The revival of this vibrant decade provides a canvas on which we can paint a future that honors our planet. By intertwining sustainability with nostalgia, we're not just revisiting the past; we're redefining it, ensuring that our renewed love affair with the 2000s paves the way for a brighter, greener future.

Ultimately, the lesson here is one of balance and innovation. Embracing the past with an eye towards sustainability invites us to enjoy the best of both worlds, celebrating the cultural milestones of the 2000s while contributing to a more sustainable and equitable planet. It's an opportunity to demonstrate that progress and nostalgia can coexist, guiding us toward a future where respecting our planet is as intrinsic to our culture as the trends we revive.

As we move forward, let's carry this spirit of sustainable innovation with us, making every decision a reflection of our commitment to a healthier planet. The 2000s brought us into a new millennium with hope and excitement. Now, we have the chance to shape this era into one marked by our efforts to safeguard the environment, ensuring that the revival of 2000s trends is remembered not just for its style and technology, but for its contribution to a sustainable world. It's a challenge we can meet with creativity, enthusiasm, and a shared vision for a greener tomorrow.

The Cyclical Nature of Culture: Predicting the Next Big Revival

Culture, in its infinite loop, brings us back to what once was, dusting off the past's relics and presenting them anew with a modern twist. As we delve further into the 21st century, the 2000s have begun to resurface, stirring a mix of nostalgia and novelty among those who lived through it and those who didn't. But what makes a culture cycle back to a particular era? And more importantly, as we stand on the brink of the 2020s, what aspects of the early 2000s are poised for a comeback, and how will they be reimagined by today's generation?

The answer lies in the unique blend of familiarity and innovation. The 2000s, with their burgeoning digital revolution, laid the groundwork for much of the technology we take for granted today. From social media's infancy to the dominance of mobile devices, the era set a precedent for the connected life we now lead. As we look to the future, we can expect a revival of 2000s tech, but with a sustainable and ethical approach that speaks to today's values.

In fashion, we've already seen hints of Y2K styles creeping back onto runways and into streetwear - low-rise jeans, cargo pants, and vibrant color palettes. Yet, as these aesthetics return, they are being infused with a consciousness of sustainability and inclusivity, challenging the fast-fashion model that dominated the era. The next

131

big revival in 2000s fashion will likely continue to blend these early millennium looks with eco-friendly materials and practices, appealing to a generation that values both style and substance.

Music from the 2000s, characterized by the rise of digital downloads and the iPod, is also witnessing a resurgence. However, today's artists are sampling 2000s hits, reinterpreting them through contemporary genres and using modern platforms like streaming services to reach audiences. This reincarnation emphasizes the emotional connection listeners had with the music of the early 2000s while introducing it to a new audience in a fresh, relevant way.

The realm of television and film is ripe for 2000s revivals, too. With streaming services now dominant, classic 2000s shows and movies are being rebooted or continued, much to the delight of original fans and new viewers alike. The approach, however, is more nuanced and reflective of today's social climate, often addressing past shortcomings in diversity and representation.

Video gaming, a rapidly evolving industry, owes much to the innovations of the 2000s. As we look ahead, expect to see games and consoles from the era reimagined with cutting-edge technology, delivering nostalgia-inducing experiences that leverage virtual reality, augmented reality, and more to create immersive gameplay that far surpasses what was possible two decades ago.

In terms of social media, the landscape has dramatically shifted since the days of MySpace and early YouTube. Yet, there's a growing interest in the digital simplicity and authenticity of 2000s internet culture. Future platforms may seek to recapture that sense of community and genuine connection, moving away from the polished, curated feeds that dominate today's social media sphere.

Beauty and body image, which underwent a narrow representation in the 2000s, are now embracing inclusivity and diversity. The next revival might bring back glittery eyeshadows and poker-straight hair, but paired with a celebration of all body types, genders, and ethnicities, pushing back against the era's often exclusive beauty standards.

Reality TV, a hallmark of the 2000s, continues to evolve. Today's versions aim to be more socially conscious, shedding light on real-world issues while maintaining the entertaining, unscripted drama that audiences love. This reflects a broader shift toward content that is both engaging and enlightening.

Environmentalism, which began gaining significant traction in the 2000s, is now a critical factor in all sectors, from fashion to technology. The revival of 2000s trends with an emphasis on sustainability reflects a collective push towards a more responsible and conscious culture.

Even the activism and social movements that defined the 2000s are experiencing a renaissance, buoyed by the power of social media to mobilize and unite. However, today's movements are more global, more inclusive, and more interconnected, demonstrating the evolution of 2000s ethos to fit a new era.

The cycle of culture brings the past forward, not to relive it exactly as it was, but to understand it, learn from it, and make it better. As we predict the next big revival, it's clear that the essence of the 2000s will be preserved, but its form will be updated to reflect the values, technology, and social consciousness of today's world.

Understanding this cyclical nature is key to appreciating the ongoing dialogue between past and present. It's not just about bringing back what we missed or romanticizing what was; it's about building bridges between generations, learning from our collective history, and moving forward with intention and awareness.

As we stand on the cusp of this new era, we're tasked with a unique opportunity: to shape the revival of the 2000s in a way that honors its legacy while propelling us towards a more inclusive, sustainable, and connected future. The cyclical nature of culture isn't just a pattern to observe—it's a process we're all a part of, actively creating and re-creating the world around us.

In embracing the next big revival, we're not just looking back; we're looking forward, armed with the knowledge of the past and the vision to make the future our own. The 2000s, with all their complexity, excitement, and innovation, offer a rich tapestry from which we can draw inspiration, learn lessons, and forge a new path that reflects where we've been and where we hope to go.

Gen Z and Millennials: Bridging the Past with the Future

The dawn of the new millennium was more than just a calendar flip; it marked the beginning of a cultural evolution, one that shaped the identities of both Millennials and Gen Z. The 2000s were a vibrant era, characterized by rapid technological advancements, distinctive fashion trends, memorable music, and groundbreaking television shows. Today, as we gaze into the future, the question arises: How are Gen Z and Millennials bridging the past with the future, and what implications does this have for our cultural landscape?

Firstly, it's essential to acknowledge the unique circumstances that define each generation. Millennials, born roughly between 1981 and 1996, came of age during the rise of the internet, experiencing firsthand the transition from analog to digital. Gen Z, born from 1997 onward, entered a world where digital technology was already integrated into daily life. Despite their different starting points, both generations share a collective nostalgia for the 2000s, albeit interpreted through different lenses.

One of the most visible bridges between the past and the future is fashion. The resurgence of Y2K styles—low-rise jeans, cargo pants, and butterfly clips—spearheaded by social media platforms like Instagram and TikTok, reflects a yearning for the simplicity and boldness of early 2000s fashion. However, this isn't merely replication. Today's renditions are often imbued with contemporary values of inclusivity and sustainability, repurposing vintage finds and advocating for ethical production practices.

Music, too, plays a crucial role in linking generations. Gen Z has rediscovered 2000s pop icons, emo bands, and punk rock music, drawing parallels between the angst and rebellion expressed in early 2000s music and the societal challenges they face today. This resurgence isn't just about nostalgia; it's about finding solace and understanding in the melodies and lyrics that once defined a generation.

The realm of entertainment, particularly television and movies, also illustrates the bridge between past and future. Streaming services have breathed new life into 2000s sitcoms and dramas, allowing Gen Z to experience these cultural phenomena on their terms. Furthermore, the revival of beloved franchises and the rebooting of classic shows offer a shared space for Millennials and Gen Z to connect over mutual interests.

In the sphere of technology, both generations have witnessed the shift from analog to digital in their formative years. This shared experience fosters a unique bond, as both cohorts appreciate the rapid evolution of technology while reminiscing about the simplicity of early internet days. The nostalgic appeal of flip phones and early social media platforms contrasts sharply with today's sleek smartphones and sophisticated online environments, prompting discussions about the implications of technological progress.

Importantly, the collaboration between Gen Z and Millennials is evident in their approach to activism and social awareness. Both generations value authenticity and are quick to leverage digital platforms for advocacy. The environmental campaigns, social justice movements, and push for inclusivity that began in the 2000s have found renewed vigor among these cohorts, who utilize their collective voice and technological savvy to effect change.

This bridge between past and future is also evident in the gaming industry. Classic 2000s video games and consoles are experiencing a renaissance, driven by both nostalgia and the desire for simpler, more straightforward gameplay amidst today's complex gaming landscape. This shared interest in gaming has fostered a unique camaraderie, with online communities and multiplayer experiences transcending generational divides.

Beauty and fashion trends from the 2000s are being revisited with a modern twist, reflecting changing attitudes towards body image and representation. Today's reinterpretations emphasize diversity and body positivity, marking a significant evolution from the past's often narrow standards of beauty.

The influence of 2000s reality TV on contemporary media cannot be overlooked. Gen Z, in particular, consumes reality TV with a critical eye, understanding both its entertainment value and its impact on perception and social dynamics. This critical consumption sparks conversations about media literacy and the role of entertainment in shaping societal norms.

Moreover, the shared digital space has allowed for an amalgamation of 2000s internet culture with modern online phenomena. Viral challenges, memes, and social media trends often draw inspiration from the past, recontextualized for today's digital audience. This blending of eras fosters a unique sense of community and continuity among users across the generational spectrum.

As we navigate the complexities of the present and look towards the future, the collaborative efforts of Gen Z and Millennials in reinterpreting 2000s culture underscore a deeper yearning for connection, authenticity, and understanding. By bridging the past with the future, these generations are not only preserving cultural artifacts but are also shaping a future that values inclusivity, sustainability, and genuine expression.

Thus, in a world that often feels dominated by uncertainty and rapid change, the 2000s serve as a touchstone for both Millennials and Gen Z. It is a reminder of simpler times while providing a foundation for exploring new frontiers. From fashion to technology, music to activism, the imprints of the 2000s continue to influence our collective journey, inspiring us to reimagine the past in ways that inform our approach to the future.

In conclusion, as we stand at the crossroads of history, the relationship between Millennials, Gen Z, and the 2000s cultural legacy is a testament to the enduring power of nostalgia mixed with innovation. It is a bridge across time, uniting past and future, and reminding us that even as we forge ahead, our roots remain a source of strength, wisdom, and inspiration. The journey ahead is bright, with the past as our guide and the future ours to shape.

Chapter 13:
Millennium Redux - Embracing the Past, Influencing the Future

As we draw the curtains on a journey through time, revisiting the echoes of the early 2000s, it's evident that this era left an indelible mark on us. The revival isn't merely a nostalgic trip down memory lane but a powerful testament to the 2000s' enduring influence on culture, technology, and society. At its heart, this resurgence is a narrative of how the past informs the present, shaping a future that nods respectfully to its origins.

The 2000s were a time of rapid change, a period when technology and culture collided in unprecedented ways. As we traced the arc of this era's return, we saw the threads of the past reweaved into the fabric of today's society. Fashion trends that dominated the early part of the millennium have made their way back onto runways and sidewalks, not as mere replicas but as evolved versions that reflect contemporary values and aspirations.

Technology, too, has felt the pulse of this revival. The gadgets and platforms that defined the 2000s' digital landscape have given way to advanced iterations that build on the legacy of their predecessors. From flip phones making a comeback as fashion statements to the resurgence of vinyl and mixtapes in digital formats, the tech trends of the 2000s are celebrated and reinvented for a new generation.

The music and media that shaped the turn of the millennium continue to resonate, finding new life through streaming services and social media platforms. Icons of the era are revisited and revered, their work influencing a new wave of artists and creators. In the same vein, the television shows and movies that captured the zeitgeist of the 2000s are being rebooted and reimagined, connecting audiences old and new with stories that transcend time.

This renaissance is not without its critical assessments. As the 2000s are reinterpreted for today's context, there's a concerted effort to address the shortcomings of the past. Discussions around inclusivity, diversity, and sustainability reflect a generation that is keen to take the best of the past and improve upon it for a fairer and more equitable future.

Moreover, the resurgence of the 2000s has opened up a dialogue between generations. Millennials, who lived through the era as teens and young adults, find themselves revisiting their youth, while Gen Z discovers these trends anew. This intergenerational exchange enriches the cultural landscape, allowing for a fusion of perspectives and experiences that is both innovative and reflective.

The revival of the 2000s is not just about looking back but about moving forward with intention. It's about recognizing the impact of this pivotal decade on our collective consciousness and leveraging it to shape a future that honors diversity, creativity, and connectivity. As we blend the aesthetics and values of the past with the technologies and possibilities of the present, we carve out a new trajectory that is informed by where we've been and inspired by where we're going.

The fashion, music, technology, and media of the 2000s served as a backdrop to a time of exploration and innovation. Revisiting these elements today encourages a reevaluation of what we cherished and why, urging us to preserve what is valuable and to discard what no longer serves us. In this way, the 2000s revival is a discerning process, a deliberate act of curating the past to inform a more thoughtful and inclusive future.

As we embrace the past, we're also reminded of the capacity for change, for growth, and for reinterpretation. The 2000s revival isn't about a simple reproduction of what was but a complex negotiation of what could be. It's a dynamic interplay between memory and innovation, a dance between nostalgia and aspiration.

This journey through the 2000s and its resurgence has highlighted the cyclical nature of culture. Trends may come and go, but the underlying human desires for connection, expression, and understanding remain constant. By looking back, we gain insights into our collective desires and fears, using them as a beacon to guide us forward.

The future of the 2000s, as we've seen, is not a fixed point but a continuum. It's an evolving narrative that we all contribute to, shaped by our actions, our creativity, and our vision. As we stand at this unique crossroads, with one foot in the past and one in the future, we're afforded a rare opportunity to build a bridge between eras, crafting a legacy that is as much about where we're headed as it is about where we've been.

In this millennium redux, we're not just passive observers but active participants. We have the power to influence the future by the choices we make today, by the trends we embrace, the values we uphold, and the narratives we craft. It's a call to action, an invitation to engage with our history, not as a relic of the past but as a living, breathing blueprint for the future.

As we continue to explore and reinterpret the 2000s, we do so with the knowledge that we're not merely revisiting a time gone by but reimagining a world yet to be. This era, with all its complexities and contradictions, offers a fertile ground for innovation, a canvas on which to paint our hopes, dreams, and aspirations for the decades to come.

In embracing the past and influencing the future, we embark on a journey of discovery and renewal. The millennium redux is not just a cultural phenomenon but a movement, a testament to the enduring power of human creativity and resilience. As we move forward, guided by the lessons and legacies of the 2000s, we do so with optimism, courage, and the unwavering belief that the best is yet to come.

Appendix A:
Resources for 2000s Culture Enthusiasts

If the journey through the 2000s has reignited a spark in you, this appendix is your next step towards exploring the depths of this unique era. Whether you're a millennial feeling the sting of nostalgia or a Gen Z'er curious about the cultural phenomena that shaped the early part of the millennium, the resources listed here will help you dive deeper into the 2000s culture. Let's keep the nostalgia alive and explore more about the fashion, music, technology, and social movements that defined a generation.

Reading List

Dive into these recommended reads to gain a deeper understanding of the 2000s:

- **"The Tipping Point: How Little Things Can Make a Big Difference" by Malcolm Gladwell** - Understand the social dynamics that led to the virality of trends in the 2000s.

- **"Styling Masculinity: Gender, Class, and Inequality in the Men's Grooming Industry" by Kristen Barber** - Explore the evolution of men's fashion and grooming in the 2000s.

- **"Retromania: Pop Culture's Addiction to Its Own Past" by Simon Reynolds** - Offers insight into why we're so obsessed with cultural revivals, including the 2000s resurgence.

Online Archives and Websites

These online havens are goldmines for 2000s culture:

- *Y2K Aesthetic Institute (Tumblr)* - An archive dedicated to the visual culture of the late 90s and early 2000s, from fashion to technology.

- *Internet Archive (archive.org)* - Dive into web pages, videos, and music from the 2000s that have been preserved in digital amber.

- *MySpace Nostalgia (Reddit)* - Revisit the glory days of MySpace, where users share old profiles, music, and the social dynamics of early social media.

Social Media Accounts and Hashtags to Follow

For a daily dose of 2000s nostalgia, these social media accounts and hashtags will connect you to content you didn't know you needed:

- **@y2k_aesthetic** (Instagram) - This account curates the finest Y2K fashion, tech, and pop culture posts.

- **@early2000ss** (Twitter) - Flashback tweets that will transport you back to simpler times.

- **Hashtag #2000sRevival** (TikTok) - Discover video content focusing on 2000s fashion makeovers, music covers, and tech throwbacks.

In immersing yourself in these resources, remember that the 2000s were more than just a decade; they were a launchpad for today's cultural, technological, and social phenomena. By exploring these resources, you're not just revisiting the past; you're understanding the roots of our present, preparing to shape a future that respects diversity, inclusivity, and innovation. Let the 2000s be more than a memory; let them inspire a future where we carry forward the best of what we've learned, loved, and lived.

Reading List

For those captivated by the shimmer and shadow of the 2000s, the era isn't just a bygone period; it's a rich tapestry of culture, technology, and style awaiting rediscovery. As we delve into the Reading List section, we uncover a curated collection of books that serve not only as gateways to the past but also as lenses through which we can view the resurgence of 2000s trends with fresh eyes. This compilation is carefully designed for enthusiasts eager to explore the depths of an era that shaped the turn of the millennium, influencing not just Millennials but also piquing the curiosity of Gen Z.

First on our list is a deep dive into the heart of 2000s pop culture. This book explores the explosive growth of digital media, the birth of social networking sites, and the iconic fashion statements that have circled back into relevance. It's a must-read for anyone looking to understand the foundational shifts that occurred in music, television, and online spaces, reshaping entertainment as we knew it.

Another essential addition focuses on the technological advances of the 2000s, from the omnipresence of the iPod to the early days of YouTube. It sheds light on how these platforms revolutionized consumption and creation, setting the stage for today's digital landscape. This read is for those mesmerized by the rapid evolution of gadgets and the internet, offering a narrative that connects the dots between past innovations and current trends.

The sartorial shifts of the 2000s cannot be overlooked, with entire volumes dedicated to the era's fashion evolution. From denim on denim to the unforgettable rise of velour tracksuits, these books examine how 2000s fashion was influenced by celebrity culture, music videos, and the dawn of fashion blogging. They illustrate how today's runways and street styles are echoing the bold choices of the early aughts, infused with a modern sensibility.

Music enthusiasts will find solace in titles that chronicle the rise of pop icons, the resurgence of vinyl, and the mixtape culture that defined a generation. These books go beyond mere biography, delving into the emotional resonance of 2000s music, its role in shaping identity, and its lasting impact on fans and artists alike. They serve as a testament to the enduring power of melody and rhythm that continues to echo through today's hits.

Reality TV, a hallmark of the 2000s, transformed the television landscape in ways that are still being unpacked. Selected works in our list explore this phenomenon from its earnest beginnings to the spectacle it became, offering insights into how reality TV reshaped viewer engagement and blazed the trail for today's influencer culture. These reads are perfect for those fascinated by the spectacle of the real and its implications for entertainment and society.

The body image and fitness craze of the 2000s also warrant examination. Through a collection of thoughtful critiques and retrospectives, readers can explore how media representations of beauty evolved during the decade and the resulting impacts on health and self-perception. These books offer a nuanced look at the journey toward more inclusive and diverse standards of beauty that continues to unfold today.

Video game aficionados will relish in titles dedicated to the virtual playgrounds of the 2000s. From the console wars to the rise of online multiplayer games, these books capture the spirit and innovation of the gaming sphere. They highlight how these digital worlds forged communities, influenced pop culture, and laid the groundwork for the esports phenomena.

For those intrigued by the socio-political climate of the 2000s, a selection of works examines the activism and social awareness campaigns that defined the decade. From the green movement to the early days of social justice hashtags, these readings contextualize how activism in the 2000s sowed the seeds for today's global movements, emphasizing the power of collective action and digital advocacy.

Last but certainly not least, our list includes introspections on the internet culture that flourished in the 2000s. Memes, virality, niche forums — these books dissect the beginnings of online communities and the ways in which they've influenced language, humor, and human connection. They're essential for anyone curious about the lineage of our digital vernacular and the foundational roles these early web spaces played in shaping internet culture.

This reading list is crafted to guide enthusiasts through a journey back in time, offering a comprehensive understanding of an era that continues to influence our present and future. The 2000s were not just a stepping stone but a significant period of cultural and technological ferment that laid the groundwork for the world as we know it today.

As you explore these texts, you'll find yourself immersed in the nuances of a not-so-distant past, equipped to appreciate the cyclical nature of trends and the ongoing dialogue between yesterday's icons and today's influencers. This collection doesn't just revisit the past; it reinvigorates it, inviting readers to rediscover the 2000s with the wisdom of hindsight and the excitement of foresight.

Whether you're a millennial looking back on your formative years or a Gen Z'er curious about the cultural artifacts of the recent past, this reading list serves as a bridge across generations. It encourages a deeper understanding of how we've arrived at our current moment, fostering a sense of continuity and appreciation for the relentless pace of change.

In the end, this collection is more than just a series of titles; it's an invitation to explore, to learn, and to be inspired. The 2000s aren't just a period to be nostalgically remembered; they offer lessons, warnings, and inspiration for crafting the future. By looking back, we learn to move forward with intention and insight, ensuring that the best of the past is carried into the innovative and inclusive future we're building together.

So, take a journey back to the 2000s with this reading list at your side, and discover the era that shaped a generation and continues to inspire the next. It's an exploration of where we've been, how far we've come, and where we're poised to go, all through the lens of a vibrant and transformative decade.

Online Archives and Websites

In an age where digital archives and websites serve as the gatekeepers of history, enthusiasts of 2000s culture find themselves in a unique position. The turn of the millennium was a time when the internet began its shift from novelty to necessity, embedding itself into the fabric of our daily lives. For those yearning to revisit or discover the 2000s, a wealth of resources awaits online, providing an immersive dive into the era that shaped the contemporary digital world.

One of the first stops for any 2000s culture enthusiast is the Wayback Machine. This digital archive is a time capsule, allowing users to explore websites exactly as they appeared at various points in time. Imagine revisiting the original MySpace layout or the early days of Google. The nostalgia is palpable as you navigate these digital relics, offering a poignant reminder of the internet's evolution.

Dedicated forums and fan sites remain active, populated by communities who share a passion for the 2000s. From discussions about the golden age of emo music to retrospectives on early reality TV phenomena, these platforms offer deep dives into niche topics. The collective knowledge and enthusiasm of these communities provide a rich tapestry of information and insight, making them invaluable resources for both new fans and those looking to reminisce.

Blogs dedicated to 2000s pop culture have carved out their own niche in the online landscape. Authors often combine personal anecdotes with cultural analysis, offering a layered perspective on the era. Posts might explore the impact of iconic music videos, dissect the fashion trends of the early 2000s, or offer think pieces on the cultural significance of landmark films and TV shows.

YouTube channels have emerged as a vital source for experiencing 2000s culture, with users uploading content ranging from music videos and movie trailers to entire episodes of TV shows that aired during the decade. Additionally, video essays and retrospectives provide context and commentary, enriching the viewing experience with historical insight and critical analysis.

Online museums and digital exhibitions offer curated experiences focusing on 2000s art, design, and technology. These platforms often feature interactive elements, allowing visitors to engage with the material in dynamic ways. By highlighting the visual and technological trends of the time, online exhibits capture the aesthetic and mood of the era, making them a must-visit for those interested in design and tech history.

Sharing playlists and mixtapes on music streaming services has become a way to recreate the soundscapes of the 2000s. Curated collections of hits from the decade allow listeners to teleport back in time, rediscovering the songs that defined their youth or uncovering the soundtrack of an era they're just getting to know.

For those interested in the tech advances of the 2000s, there are websites dedicated to exploring the gadgets and software that began the digital revolution. From the rise of MP3 players and smartphones to the evolution of social media platforms, these sites offer a deep dive into the technological innovations that have shaped our current digital landscape.

Research archives and academic journals are also embracing digital access, providing in-depth studies and papers on various aspects of early 21st-century culture. Whether you're interested in the impact of 2000s media on societal norms or analyses of trends in digital communication, scholarly resources offer grounded, insightful perspectives.

Fashion blogs and digital lookbooks recreate the sartorial splendor of the 2000s. With a focus on everything from iconic red carpet looks to everyday attire, these resources celebrate the eclectic fashion of the era. Interactive features like 'get the look' segments allow visitors to explore how they can incorporate 2000s fashion into their contemporary wardrobes.

Virtual marketplaces and online auctions provide a tangible connection to the 2000s, with listings for vintage tech, clothing, and memorabilia. These platforms not only facilitate the acquisition of period-specific items but also help to preserve the material culture of the decade.

Online fan clubs and social media groups bring together people from around the globe, united by their appreciation for 2000s culture. These digital communities foster discussion and fan activities, from watch parties for classic 2000s films to group chats about the latest album reissues from the decade's top artists.

Digital art galleries and portfolio sites showcase the work of artists and designers who were active during the 2000s or whose current work is inspired by the era. These sites provide insight into the visual trends and creative processes that defined the decade's aesthetics, offering inspiration and appreciation for the artistic expressions of the time.

Finally, websites devoted to 2000s era gaming offer emulators, retrospectives, and forums dedicated to the consoles and video games that defined a generation. From discussions about the impact of landmark titles to guides for accessing vintage games on modern equipment, these resources are a treasure trove for gamers looking to relive or discover the era's gaming culture.

The online archives and websites dedicated to 2000s culture serve as more than mere repositories of information; they are vibrant, breathing spaces where the past and present converge. They remind us that while the 2000s may be gone, their cultural, technological, and aesthetic impacts continue to shape our world. As we navigate through these digital archives, we not only revisit the past but also gain insight into how the 2000s inform our present and inspire future innovations. In this journey, we're all students and teachers, contributors and curators, connected by our shared enthusiasm for exploring the legacy of an unforgettable era.

Social Media Accounts and Hashtags to Follow

For those of us diving deep into the vast ocean of 2000s culture, social media isn't just a tool; it's our time machine. Whether you're seeking a blast from the past or looking for ways these two decades are influencing the now, there are countless accounts and hashtags that serve as gateways to reconnecting with and reimagining the era. Let's embark on a digital journey to explore the corners of the internet where the 2000s never really ended.

Start with Instagram, where visual nostalgia reigns supreme. Accounts like @y2kaesthetic bring to life the vibrant, often neon-infused visuals that defined early digital design. Here, you'll find a curated collection of iconic fashion moments, tech gadgets that were the height of cool, and scenes from movies that shaped the era's pop culture landscape. It's a reminder of the days when flip phones were a status symbol and low-rise jeans dominated the fashion scene.

On Twitter, hashtags like #Y2KFashion and #2000sNostalgia are buzzing with discussions and memories. Users share their own throwback photos, iconic 2000s moments, and current trends that are unmistakably inspired by the era. It's a space where past and present collide, showcasing how the 2000s sensibilities are being reinterpreted by modern designers and stylists. Following these hashtags feels like joining a community where everyone shares your affection for cargo pants and frosted lip gloss.

TikTok, with its dynamic content, is the perfect platform to see 2000s culture in action. Here, users don hashtags like #Y2KAesthetic and #2000sMusic to share bite-sized videos that celebrate the era's unique vibe. From tutorial videos on achieving the perfect 2000s inspired makeup look to lip-sync battles featuring throwback hits, TikTok revives the 2000s in a way that feels fresh and relevant to today's audiences.

Pinterest, though often overlooked, is a treasure trove of 2000s aesthetics. Boards dedicated to Y2K fashion, 2000s movie posters, and retro tech gadgets provide a vast resource for anyone looking to inject a bit of the millennium's charm into their life. Whether you're planning a 2000s-themed party or just wanting to add some nostalgia to your daily look, Pinterest offers endless inspiration.

YouTube channels dedicated to 2000s culture offer deep dives into the music, movies, and moments that defined the decade. Look for creators who do documentary-style videos on early 2000s pop icons or playlists filled with the hits that once filled our MP3 players. It's a fantastic way to re-experience the music and media that shaped a generation, with the added bonus of contemporary insights and commentary.

Facebook groups like "2000s Kids Unite!" or "Y2K Aesthetics" serve as gathering spaces for enthusiasts to share memories, merchandise finds, and even organize themed events. These groups offer a sense of community and connection, bridging geographical gaps between those who hold the 2000s dear.

For the avid reader and cultural observer, following bloggers who specialize in early 21st-century culture can be enlightening. These individuals often have a knack for connecting dots between then and now, offering analyses on how 2000s culture influences current trends, politics, and social behaviors. They might not always have the largest followings, but their insights can be gold mines for enthusiasts.

Don't forget LinkedIn, where professionals from the 2000s era often share their experiences and insights into the tech, fashion, and media industries of the time. It's a unique platform to understand the 2000s from a business and innovation perspective, delving into how it laid the groundwork for today's digital world.

Reddit's niche communities, or subreddits, such as r/nostalgia or r/The2000s, are hubs for sharing and discussing the minutiae of 2000s culture. From threads reminiscing about early internet culture to discussions on the era's most contentious fashion trends, Reddit offers a more interactive and community-driven approach to nostalgia.

Following the right accounts and hashtags is like opening a doorway to the past, and yet, it's also about more than just looking back. It's about understanding how the cultural output of the 2000s is being reevaluated and repurposed for a new era. It's a testament to the enduring impact of these two decades on our collective cultural psyche.

As we navigate these digital spaces, let's engage with them not just as passive observers but as active participants. Share your own memories, contribute to discussions, and maybe even post your own 2000s-inspired content. You'd be surprised at how many are eager to join the conversation and how these interactions can enrich your understanding and appreciation of the era.

The beauty of following these accounts and hashtags lies not just in nostalgia but in the vibrant community that it fosters. There's something profoundly communal about sharing a collective memory, about finding common ground in the things we once loved and still do. It's a reminder that, while the 2000s may be two decades behind us, its spirit continues to shape us in more ways than we might realize.

So delve into these social media realms with an open mind and a keen eye. You'll find that the 2000s have never really left us—they've just been waiting for us to rediscover them, celebrate them, and perhaps learn from them as we navigate the complexities of the modern world. The 2000s are calling; it's time we answered.

In the end, this journey through 2000s culture on social media is more than just a trip down memory lane. It's an exploration of how the past intersects with the present, influencing fashion, music, technology, and social movements today. By tapping into the wealth of content available at our fingertips, we're not only reliving the glory days but also gaining a deeper understanding of today's cultural landscape through the lens of the millennial era.

*Dedicated to Dawn Thompson –
Editor, Mentor, Daughter*